Contagious Christianity

A STUDY OF
FIRST THESSALONIANS

Contagious Christianity

A STUDY OF
FIRST THESSALONIANS
BIBLE STUDY GUIDE

From the Bible-teaching ministry of

Charles R. Swindoll

INSIGHT FOR LIVING

WORD PUBLISHING

Word (UK) Ltd
Milton Keynes, England

WORD BOOKS AUSTRALIA
Heathmont, Victoria, Australia

SUNDAY SCHOOL CENTRE WHOLESALE
Salt River, South Africa

ALBY COMMERCIAL ENTERPRISES PTE LTD
Scotts Road, Singapore

CONCORDE DISTRIBUTORS LTD
Havelock North, New Zealand

CROSS (HK) CO
Hong Kong

PRAISE INC
Quezon City, Philippines

These studies are based on the outlines of sermons delivered by Charles R. Swindoll. Chuck is a graduate of Dallas Theological Seminary and has served in pastorates for more than twenty-four years, including churches in Texas, New England, and California. Since 1971 he has served as senior pastor of the First Evangelical Free Church of Fullerton, California. Chuck's radio program, "Insight for Living," began in 1979. In addition to his church and radio ministries, Chuck has written twenty-three books and numerous booklets on a variety of subjects.

Chuck's outlines are expanded from the sermon transcripts and edited by Bill Watkins, a graduate of California State University at Fresno and Dallas Theological Seminary, with the assistance of Bill Butterworth, a graduate of Florida Bible College, Dallas Theological Seminary, and Florida Atlantic University. Bill Butterworth is currently the director of counseling ministries for Insight for Living.

Publisher:	Insight for Living, Fullerton, California
Creative Director:	Cynthia Swindoll
Editor:	Bill Watkins
Associate Editor:	Bill Butterworth
Editorial Assistants:	Jane Gillis, Wendy Jones, Tom Kimber, Marci Kuethen, and Karene Wells
Communications Manager:	Carla Beck
Production Supervisor:	Deedee Snyder
Production Assistant:	Linda Robertson
Production Artists:	Trina Crockett, Rhonda DiBello, and Chris Gorciak
Typographer:	Carla Randolph
Calligrapher:	Richard Stumpf
Cover Designer:	Michael Standlee
Cover:	*Sunday Morning in Sleepy Hollow,* courtesy of Paul Victorius Wholesale Prints, Charlottesville, Virginia, a division of Graphic Arts Unlimited, Inc.

Printed and bound in Great Britain by Cox and Wyman Ltd.

An album that contains twelve messages on six cassettes and corresponds to this study guide may be purchased through Insight for Living, Post Office Box 4444, Fullerton, California 92634. For information, please write for the current Insight for Living catalog or call (714) 870-9161. Canadian residents may direct their correspondence to Insight for Living Ministries, Post Office Box 2510, Vancouver, British Columbia, Canada V6B 3W7, or call (604) 272-5811. Australian residents should direct their correspondence to Insight for Living Ministries, General Post Office Box 2823EE, Melbourne, Victoria 3001. Other overseas residents should direct their correspondence to our Fullerton office.

ISBN 0-85009-170-5

Table of Contents

Contagious Christianity

The first letter of Paul's to find its way into the collection of New Testament books was 1 Thessalonians. Although rather brief, it is one of the most positive statements we can read that portrays a first-century congregation. Those Thessalonians were downright contagious!

In our day, when the church is all too often viewed with jaded, cynical eyes, this affirming letter needs to be declared. I believe you will be encouraged and challenged as we work our way through it, verse by verse.

Ultimately, I hope this study will boost the morale of many whose Christianity has begun drifting dangerously close to mediocrity. I know of few things that are better able to halt this disease than a massive dose of 1 Thessalonians taken on a daily basis.

Chuck Swindoll

Putting Truth into Action

Knowledge apart from application falls short of God's desire for His children. Knowledge must result in change and growth. Consequently, we have constructed this Bible study guide with these purposes in mind: (1) to stimulate discovery, (2) to increase understanding, and (3) to encourage application.

At the end of each lesson is a section called **Living Insights.** *There you'll be given assistance in further Bible study, and you'll be encouraged to contemplate and apply the things you've learned. This is the place where the lesson is fitted with shoe leather for your walk through the varied experiences of life.*

In wrapping up some lessons, you'll find a unit called **Digging Deeper.** *It will provide you with essential information and list helpful resource materials so that you can probe further into some of the issues raised in those studies.*

It's our hope that you'll discover numerous ways to use this tool. Some useful avenues we would suggest are personal meditation, joint discovery, and discussion with your spouse, family, work associates, friends, or neighbors. The study guide is also practical for Sunday school classes, Bible study groups, and, of course, as a study aid for the "Insight for Living" radio broadcast.

In order to derive the greatest benefit from this process, we suggest that you record your responses to the lessons in a notebook where writing space is plentiful. In view of the kinds of questions asked, your notebook may become a journal filled with your many discoveries and commitments. We anticipate that you will find yourself returning to it periodically for review and encouragement.

Bill Watkins
Editor

Bill Butterworth
Associate Editor

Contagious Christianity

A STUDY OF
FIRST THESSALONIANS

A Church with the Right Stuff
1 Thessalonians 1:1-10

Emerging from ancient Macedonia was a dynamic body of people who lived in the busy, free, affluent metropolis of Thessalonica. This town's citizens were influential, its economy was stable, and its location along the earliest known "freeway"—*Via Egnatia*—was enviable. Goods from the east and the west poured into this city. In its heyday, when the population was around two hundred thousand, some consideration was given to making Thessalonica, rather than Constantinople, the "capital" of the world. In the first century A.D., the evangelist and apostle Paul ventured into Thessalonica and, during a brief visit, formed a body of believers there who comprised the city's first Christian church. And what a dynamic group they were! With determination, zeal, confidence, and a Pauline style, they proclaimed the good news of Christ like thunder rolling through a canyon. As we shall see through our study of 1 Thessalonians, these first-century saints were models of authentic Christianity. They made Christianity contagious to many in their day. As a result, the example they left us is worthy of our attention and appropriation.

I. Realism: Key to a Balanced Perspective.

There is a fine line between healthy admiration and unhealthy exaltation. It's one thing to look upon a person or place with genuine respect and delight, but it's another thing to exaggerate the greatness of an individual or location. We want to honestly and fairly assess Thessalonica, the Christians who lived there, and the apostle who gave them their start. In so doing, we will strip away the veneer of idealism and discover the realistic heart of this ancient yet timeless letter. God has inspired and preserved it so that we can understand and apply it, not just be awestruck by it. So let's begin to achieve a proper perspective by getting an overview of the founder of the Thessalonian church, the city in which it existed, and the situation that prompted the writing of 1 Thessalonians.

A. The Founder. The Apostle Paul founded the church at Thessalonica. However, contrary to what many think today, he was not a superevangelist, a flawless church planter, or a

1

dynamic speaker. The common opinion about Paul in his own day was conveyed in these words: " 'His letters are weighty and strong, but his personal presence is unimpressive, and his speech contemptible' " (2 Cor. 10:10). One ancient writer described Paul as "a man small of stature, with a bald head and crooked legs, in a good state of body, with eyebrows meeting and nose somewhat hooked."[1] These comments should tell us that God's strength is best manifested through human weakness and that His greatness is usually exhibited in humility. Paul could not sway the masses with impressive speeches and a charismatic presence, but he could be a willing, tireless servant of the living God. It was approximately one year after a three-to five-week stay in Thessalonica that Paul wrote this first letter to the Thessalonian Christians. His purpose for writing it was to affirm, exhort, and teach them.

B. The City. As stated earlier, Thessalonica was a thriving metropolis in the first century. Indeed, even today it is one of the largest cities in modern Greece, though it bears a new name—Salonika, or Thessaloniki.

C. The Situation. Paul wrote this letter while he was in the middle of his second missionary journey. He had left Thessalonica and, after a short stop in Athens, moved on to Corinth (see Acts 17-18). No doubt, Paul had heard reports on the progress of the Thessalonian church which had caused him to reflect on his time with them. So, from Corinth, he penned this letter, probably the first of his recorded letters, around A.D. 50.

II. Balance: Secret of a Committed Congregation.

As we move through 1 Thessalonians, it will quickly become apparent that the recipients of this letter were not given to extremes—they managed to maintain balance in their spiritual walk with God. With this in mind, let's work our way through the first ten verses of this correspondence.

A. Greeting (v. 1). Although Paul composed this letter, he did it in conjunction with Silvanus (the Roman form of the name Silas) and Timothy. These three were colleagues in Corinth, and they had been active in the establishment of the Thessalonian church (Acts 17:1-4, 1 Thess. 3:1-2). They sent the letter *"to* the church of the Thessalonians" (emphasis added). The preposition *to* tells us that truth did not come from the church; the church did not dictate truth. Rather, the church in the New Testament was a recipient and student of the truth that the Holy

1. Onesiphorus of Iconium, *Acts of Paul and Thecla 3.*

Spirit taught through His human mouthpieces. Today, the situation is similar: When the Scriptures are taught, the church is to prick up its ears and listen; then it should obey and proclaim what it hears. Also observe that Paul gives the heavenly address for the Thessalonian church. He says that it is "in God the Father and the Lord Jesus Christ." Once individuals trust in Christ for their salvation, they are transferred from the domain of darkness to the kingdom of light (Col. 1:12-13). They become citizens in God's forever kingdom, and they can never lose their citizenship (cf. John 10:27-29, Rom. 8:31-39). Now, since this is true, citizens of God's kingdom are expected to live a certain way. Their lives are to be marked by grace and peace.

B. Thanking (v. 2). After this brief opening, Paul turns to giving thanks: "We give thanks to God always for all of you, making mention of you in our prayers." How easy and enjoyable it is to pray for people who give us reason to be grateful! They often prove to be accepting and affirming, real instead of phony, and supportive and giving rather than subversive and grabby. Just as the Thessalonians gave Paul reason to be thankful for them, we should also give others reason to be grateful for our presence in their lives.

C. Remembering (vv. 3-5). Paul specified three things about the Thessalonian believers that caused him to regularly remember them in prayer. First was their "work of faith"—that is, their good works that flowed from their Christian faith. Second was their "labor of love" or, put another way, their active toiling that was prompted by their love. And third was their "steadfastness of hope"—their ability to persevere under the pressures of life because their hope was fixed on the Lord Jesus Christ. These first-century Christians did not hide their Christianity or try to live in isolation from one another. Instead, they worked together to incarnate their faith to a disbelieving, antagonistic world. Notice that they could do this because they knew that they were no longer under God's wrath but were now "beloved by God," chosen by Him for salvation (v. 4). And this was possible because the gospel was presented to them not "in word only, but also in power and in the Holy Spirit [the divine side] and with full conviction [the human side]" (v. 5a). Paul and his companions brought the good news of Christ to the Thessalonians with the firm belief that it was true (Acts 17:1-3) and with the caring desire to live it out before them (1 Thess. 1:5b, 2:8-12). They came with answers and vulnerability. They clothed the gospel with human skin, not simply verbal air.

D. Affirming (vv. 6-8). In these verses Paul affirmed the Thessalonian Christians for two responses they made to the gospel message. The first words of encouragement concern *their personal modeling of the gospel before other Christians:* "You also became imitators [mimics] of us and of the Lord, having received [or welcomed] the word in much tribulation with the joy of the Holy Spirit, so that you became an example to all the believers in Macedonia and in Achaia" (vv. 6-7). The second affirmation was given because of *the vigor with which they proclaimed the gospel to non-Christians:* "For the word of the Lord has sounded forth from you . . . in every place your faith toward God has gone forth, so that we have no need to say anything" (v. 8). People even far away from Thessalonica had heard the good news about Christ because a group of Christians in one locale had taken the initiative to get the word out to every place they could. Obviously, they had the right stuff. They did such a good job that Paul could hardly utter a word wherever they had been without someone saying, "Some Thessalonians already gave us that message." How quickly the gospel would spread today if each Christian would simply do what the Thessalonians did so many hundreds of years ago!

E. Reporting (vv. 9-10). Wherever Paul went, people told him of the change that they saw among several individuals in Thessalonica. They reported to him how many Thessalonians had "turned to God from idols to serve a living and true God" (v. 9). That is, they turned from what was dead and led to everlasting death to what is alive and leads to everlasting life. These believers also expectedly waited for the coming of Christ from heaven (v. 10). In summary, the Thessalonian Christians manifested the responsibility to take the truth to the lost and to live out the truth among the saved. They also displayed their anticipation of Christ's return without becoming complacent in their Christian responsibilities.

III. Commitment: Challenge for a Growing Christian.

From this brief portion of Scripture, we can readily see that the Thessalonian Christians had the right stuff. They exemplified balanced commitment tempered by realism in their spiritual lives. We, too, can have what they had, but it cannot be achieved without commitment. A good place to start is to make the same commitments that the ancient Thessalonians clearly made. Let's look at them together and make them an essential part of our Christian lives.

A. Commit yourself to *Christians* by standing ready to accept and support them.

B. Commit yourself to *non-Christians* by remaining available to meet their needs with your words and your life.

C. Commit yourself to *Christ* by staying free of any entanglements that keep you from living each day as if it were your last.

1 Thessalonians: A Heart-to-Heart Talk

WRITER: Paul, the Apostle
DATE: Early, probably about A.D. 50
KEY PASSAGES: 1:8-10, 4:9-11
BACKGROUND: Acts 17:1-9

UNIQUE CONTRIBUTIONS
- First of Paul's letters
- Sets forth his style of ministry
- Provides insight into the Rapture of the Church
- Offers needed balance regarding the Lord's imminent return
- Emphasis on vocational diligence

	THE PASTOR'S HEART...			THE PASTOR'S BURDEN...
Thanksgiving	The Pastor before the Flock	Personal Concern	Sexual Purity	Stay Alert!
Remembering				Encourage One Another!
Affirming	The Flock's Response to Him	Comfort and Relief	Prophetic Urgency	Live in Peace!
Reporting				
Chapter 1	Chapter 2	Chapter 3	Chapter 4	Chapter 5

PERSPECTIVE	LOOKING BACK		THE OCCASION	THE CONCERN	LOOKING AHEAD	
SUBJECT	THE CHURCH ITSELF	THE MAN HIMSELF	THE OCCASION	THE CONCERN	THE BALANCE	
ESPECIALLY APPROPRIATE FOR...	...NEW CONVERTS	...YOUNG PASTORS	...SUFFERING CHRISTIANS	...TEMPTED AND UNINFORMED CHRISTIANS	...SLEEPY CHRISTIANS	

© 1982 Charles R. Swindoll

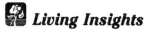 *Living Insights*

Study One

As soon as you read the title of this series and the title of this message, you know we're dealing with a church that is one exciting group! Let's probe further into this book to see why it was so contagious with the right stuff.

- Take a few minutes to read through 1 Thessalonians. Make a copy of the following chart in your own notebook. As you read, look for qualities described in the letter that are worthy of following in your life (some examples in chapter 1, verse 3 are the work of faith, the labor of love, and the steadfastness of hope). Write these traits down in the left column of the chart, putting the accompanying Scripture reference in the right column.

1 Thessalonians: Qualities of Contagious Christians	
Qualities	References

 Living Insights

Study Two

Realism, balance, and commitment . . . only three of the many ways to describe those contagious Thessalonian believers. Let's rethink our list of qualities from study one.

- After taking a look back at the list of qualities of a contagious Christian, how would you measure yourself? Try this little system to clarify your thoughts. If you're doing a good job in a particular trait, put a star (★) next to it in the left margin of your chart. If you're doing okay, write "OK" next to it. Now, in those areas of weakness, put a check (√) in the margin. How can you strengthen these areas of your life? Spend some time thinking it through on a personal level. The effort you put into this will be well worth it.

A Leadership Style that Works . . . *Guaranteed!*

1 Thessalonians 2:1-12

Our world abounds with information on the subject of leadership. This data is communicated through films, video tapes, records, cassette tapes, seminars, conferences, and books . . . all designed to help us become better leaders. Sometimes the promises conveyed are true. However, more often than not, we are simply left with another set of techniques that leaves us frustrated and overwhelmed rather than free and confident. Furthermore, these numerous materials seldom take us to the Scriptures to discover what God has to say about leadership. In this lesson, we want to depart from the norm and turn to God's Word for the direction we need. Here our model is a man whom God used to capture the hearts of a group of people who lived in ancient Greece. After ministering to them for about one month, this individual left these people unified, enthusiastic, and prepared to carry on in his absence. The man? Paul the apostle. The people? The Thessalonians.

I. A Brief Comment about Leadership.

If there is one ingredient that is essential to the success of an organization, it is leadership. Whether it is a business, church, athletic team, military unit, home, or whatever, the secret of progress usually rests with those who are in charge—the leaders. Since leadership is so important, we need to be clear about what it is.

   A. A Definition. Succinctly stated, *leadership* is "inspiring influence." Those who lead others with the greatest degree of success are able to light the spark that prompts others toward cooperation, hard work, and, if necessary, personal sacrifice.

   B. A Clarification. Given this singular *definition* of leadership, we should not assume that there is only one *style* of leadership. Some people are hard-charging, prima-donna-like leaders who rely almost exclusively on extrinsic motivation. Others lead in a very laid-back and quiet fashion, never raising their voices above a conversational tone. Yet both styles can be equally effective and inspiring. Effective leaders can be found with all different kinds of temperaments. But there is one key ingredient they are not without—*the ability to get along with people.* A leader cannot be successful unless he can deal well with people. Intelligence, decisiveness, job knowledge, technical skills . . . no other factor makes as great a difference as this one.

II. A Leadership Style Rarely Explained and Seldom Modeled.

As we turn our focus to 1 Thessalonians 2:1-12, let's begin by getting our bearings with some background material.

8

A. Historical Background (vv. 1-2). In chapters 1 and 2, Paul periodically reminds his readers about things of which they are well aware (1:5, 2:1-2, 5, 9-11). Among these reminders is the fact that his coming to them was "not in vain" (2:1). His visit had not been unfruitful or unproductive. It had purpose and had accomplished many significant things. He also reminds them that when he and his companions arrived in Thessalonica, they had "already suffered and been mistreated in Philippi" (v. 2a). Luke records that Paul and Silas were disrobed, beaten with rods, and imprisoned in Philippi (Acts 16:12, 22-24). But Paul was able to say that, even after such a physical and emotional ordeal, "we had the boldness in our God to speak to you the gospel of God amid much opposition" (1 Thess. 2:2b).

A Personal Note: More often than not, the best leaders come from a scarred past. They can lead more effectively because they have come to personally understand suffering, ill-treatment, and opposition. If you have a disability, it need not disqualify you from leadership. A crippling disease . . . a memory of sexual abuse . . . a broken home . . . a criminal record . . . financial bankruptcy . . . nothing needs to render you incapable of leading others. In fact, such trying experiences can develop you into an even better leader because they drive home to you the value of hope. A prime function of a leader is to keep hope alive in those whom he or she leads. Like Paul, your disabilities and struggles may be the seasoning you need to make you into the best leader you can possibly be.

B. Some Negatives: Things to Omit (vv. 3-6). In these verses, Paul suggests four traits that should *not* characterize a Christian leader. He accomplishes this by opening himself up for scrutiny.

    1. Deception (v. 3). Paul states, "For our exhortation does not come from error or impurity or by way of deceit." Paul is claiming that when he and his companions came to minister in Thessalonica, they did not exercise their leadership with any hidden agenda or from any faulty motives. Instead, they were sincere and pure. They were what they appeared to be. In a word, they had *integrity.*

    2. People-pleasing (v. 4). Continuing, Paul says, "but just as we have been approved by God to be entrusted with the gospel, so we speak, not as pleasing men but God, who examines our hearts." While good leaders are people-oriented, they should not be people-pleasers or flatterers. Indeed, the attempt to make everyone happy at any cost is usually a sign of insecurity. Christians who lead should not be people-pleasers but God-pleasers. They need to come to the place where the most important thing is keeping God's principles and striving after His goals. Without God at the center of their lives, they will never be successful servants of Christ. Paul makes this point quite clearly: "For am I now seeking the favor of men, or of God? Or am I striving to please men? If I were still trying to please men, I would not be a bond-servant of Christ" (Gal. 1:10). We cannot focus on pleasing Christ and strive to please people at the same time. However, by pleasing Christ we can rest assured that we will be doing what is best for people.

3. Greed (v. 5). Paul mentions this negative in these words: "For we never came with flattering speech, as you know, nor with a pretext for greed—God is witness." Greed is the desire to possess more than one needs. When taken to the extreme, greed is the desire to possess that which belongs to someone else. A person can be greedy for any number of things, including money, glory, results, attendance, facilities, and popularity. There can even be a greed for truth—an attitude that says, "I want more of the truth than anyone else." It's not that any of these things are bad in themselves. Instead, the problem lies in the insatiable drive to have something in greater abundance than anyone else. This drive takes our focus off of God and puts us in an unhealthy competition with other people. We do not need to fall into this trap. In fact, we can combat greed through the exercise of frugality, anonymity, and moderation. Self-control should characterize all our lives—especially those of us who are leaders. Greed is a sign that the leader has lost self-control.

4. Authoritarianism (v. 6). Furthermore, Paul adds that they did not "seek glory from men, either from you or from others, even though as apostles of Christ we might have asserted our authority." Paul knew that at any time he could have pulled rank on the Thessalonians. He could have used his position as an apostle and intimidated them into giving him anything he desired. But he did not abuse that authority. Instead, he came to them as a servant. His goal was to meet their needs in the best way possible. And he sought to do this without grabbing for personal glory and applause. Instead, vulnerability and transparency marked his life of service to the Thessalonians.

C. Some Positives: Things to Include (vv. 7-11). What traits *should* a leader possess? Paul suggests four in these verses.

1. Sensitivity to Needs (v. 7). Paul's words state it well: "But we proved to be gentle among you, as a nursing mother tenderly cares for her own children." There is no brush stroke of selfishness in the picture painted here. A mother is deeply committed to meeting the basic needs of her children. Also, unlike anyone else, a mother can sense the needs of her children even when they are not evident to others. Leaders should try to cultivate this same kind of selfless, sensitive, and tender care for those who follow them.

2. **Affection for People** (v. 8a). Paul remarked that he had a "fond affecton" for the Thessalonians. He treated people not as means to an end but as ends who were valuable in and of themselves. He was not cool and distant, but warm and close. In like manner, leaders should love people and manifest their love in practical and appropriate ways.

3. **Authenticity of Life** (vv. 8b-10). Paul and his companions in ministry imparted not only the gospel but also their own lives. They lived out what they proclaimed without erecting barriers that would make them aloof. They were transparent and authentic, just as leaders today should be.

4. **Enthusiastic in Affirmation** (v. 11). Paul compared two aspects of his leadership style with parenting. First, as already mentioned, he noted that leaders must have the tenderness of a mother. In verse 11, he compares leaders to fathers: "You know how we were exhorting and encouraging and imploring each one of you as a father would his own children." A good father will continue to encourage and affirm his children through their tasks, no matter what. People need this kind of enthusiastic support as well. But leaders sometimes forget this. In their push to get a job done, they can become oppressive and degrading. Christ, the greatest leader of all, never did this. Just prior to His ascension, He gathered His disciples and placed the future of Christianity into their hands (Matt. 28:16-20). In so doing, He affirmed His confidence in them—an act that resulted in the world being turned upside down by a small group of imperfect men.

D. **The Ultimate Objective** (v. 12). The major, overall objective of Paul's leadership in Thessalonica was that the Thessalonians would "walk in a manner worthy of the God" who called them into His kingdom and glory. Paul led to benefit others, not himself. He wanted what was best for His followers. He was not out to exalt himself or to use others to enhance or fulfill his own plans. If Christian leaders would make the good of their followers their ultimate objective, what a remarkable change would occur in the Church of Jesus Christ!

III. Three Essential Qualities.

If you are serious about having a lasting impact on others—no matter what capacity of leadership you find yourself in or aspire to—then you need to develop and maintain the following qualities that emerge from these verses.

A. You must develop a deep, abiding inner security. This will keep you from focusing your attention on pleasing people rather than God.

B. You must make a persistent commitment to excellence. No matter what happens, and regardless of anyone else's desire, you need to make it a point to always do your best.

C. You must make a deliberate step of faith in God. You don't stumble into a wholehearted commitment to God; you must willfully decide that you will give Christ the position that He deserves in your life—number one over all things and all people.

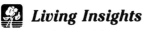 *Living Insights*

Study One ━━

We boiled down the definition of leadership to a couple of words—*inspiring influence.* The Thessalonian believers were fortunate indeed to observe Paul's leadership style firsthand! Let's take a look at a particular incident recorded in the book of Acts.

• Acts 17:1-9 tells the story of Paul's visit to Thessalonica. Make a copy of the following chart; then read through the Acts passage. Write down your own observations of Paul's leadership style and jot down the appropriate references. Conclude your study by summarizing your observations in two or three principles of leadership.

Paul's Leadership Style—Acts 17:1-9	
Reference	Observations

Principles of Leadership:

13

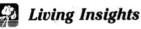 *Living Insights*

This passage in Acts details a leadership style rarely explained and seldom modeled. Whether you consider yourself a leader or not, let's do a self-evaluation. Fill in this "report card" of your leadership qualities.

● Next to each topic, give yourself a letter grade, like a teacher would on a report card. A + is best; F is worst. Take a few lines to explain why you graded yourself the way you did. Be honest, fair, and objective. Don't be too hard on yourself, but don't be too easy either!

My Leadership Report Card		
Subject	Grade	Reason
Some Negatives: Things to Omit		
—Deception		
—People-pleasing		
—Greed		
—Authoritarianism		
Some Positives: Things to Include		
—Sensitivity to Needs		
—Affection for People		
—Authenticity of Life		
—Enthusiasm in Affirmation		

The Flip Side of Leadership

1 Thessalonians 2:13-20

Your leadership skills can be tested by taking a quick glance over your shoulder: Is anyone following? A coach without a team is in a holding pattern. A salesperson with no customers accomplishes little. A teacher minus students lacks any concrete gauge for his or her motivational skills. What good are leaders without followers? And what good is the possession of quality leadership skills if the response of the followers is indifference or even resistance? Truly, the flip side of leading is *following*. And that's primarily what we are going to focus on in this study.

I. Review and Reminder.

Probably one reason Paul was so fond of the Thessalonian believers was that they were such great followers. Indeed, seldom will we ever find great leaders without also discovering that they have great followers. But before we examine the issue of following, let's make a brief excursion back to the subject of leadership dealt with in 1 Thessalonians 2:1-12.

A. Why is some leadership "not in vain"? Why do some leaders produce lasting fruit while others do not? With regard to his own ministry among the Thessalonians, Paul gives us four negatives and four positives in answer to that question. His leadership was not in vain because he refused to rely on deception, he chose not to please men over God, he served without greed, and he refused to lead in an authoritarian manner. On the positive side, Paul's leadership was characterized by a sensitivity to needs, an affection for his followers, an authenticity of life, and an enthusiastic, affirming response to those he led.

B. What good is leadership without "witnesses"? Notice that in verse 5 Paul says that God witnessed his leadership, while in verse 10 he says that the Thessalonians were his witnesses. When we lead well, not only does God applaud and support our efforts, but our followers do so as well. Our attempts at leading will never go unnoticed, and they will always impact someone. The only question is, Will they impact others for good or ill? Let's take a look at Paul's leadership and the response he received from the Thessalonians.

II. The Reason for Gratitude (1 Thessalonians 2:13a).

Paul openly expressed his gratitude for the Thessalonian Christians: "And for this reason we also constantly thank God that when you received from us the word of God's message, you accepted it." The Thessalonians received the good news about Christ as one would welcome a friend into his or her home. It's one thing to hear God's Word as it is proclaimed, but it is quite another to welcome it into one's lfe. Followers (and leaders) need to both hear and receive divine truth.

III. Some Responses in Attitude (1 Thessalonians 2:13b-20). There are some responsive attitudes that are essential for followers and others that are necessary for leaders. Let's consider them in the order Paul presents them.

    A. Among Those Being Led (vv. 13b-16). Why is it so important that followers welcome biblical teaching into the inner sanctum of their lives? Because when it is received in this way, it will effect change (v. 13b). The Spirit of God will take the seed of God's Word and plant it in the fertile soil of a willing heart. With the proper care and nourishment, in time it will take root, grow, and bear fruit, even in the worst of rebels (cf. 1 Tim. 1:12-16). But these changes cannot occur without the proper responsive attitudes. Paul lists them for us.

        1. Cooperation with Needed Changes. As the Word of God gets rooted in our lives and begins to do a work, we must be willing to make the necessary changes to allow this work to come to full fruition (v. 13b).

        2. The Imitation of a Godly Lifestyle. This attitude follows on the heels of the first one. Look at verse 14a: "For you, brethren, became imitators of the churches of God in Christ Jesus that are in Judea." The Thessalonian Christians, without ever meeting the believers in Judea, began to live a lifestyle that was similar to theirs. It's not that the Thessalonians began to give up their cultural distinctives, but rather that they began to give birth to a distinctly Christlike life. When the Lord saves us, He begins to perform a work in us that is modeled after His own Son, Jesus Christ.

        3. Endurance through Intense Sufferings. Lest you think that the Christian life will be a bed of roses, observe what Paul says: "For you also endured the same sufferings at the hands of your own countrymen, even as they did from the Jews" (v. 14). Christians have always suffered, and they will continue to suffer. That's not in doubt. The only uncertainty is how intense the suffering will be for each believer. But regardless of the degree to which any of us will experience pain and hurt, God will help us to endure it. The Lord will also make sure that those who afflict us will experience His wrath once they "fill up the measure of their sins" (v. 16b). That is, God has set limits to the sins that can be committed against each one of us. And once those limitations are met, divine discipline and judgment are carried out against those who are striking at us. The sovereign Lord always has things under control, even when we have a difficult time seeing that. This should give us, as His followers, a sense of peace.

B. Within the Leader Himself (vv. 17-20). Paul now switches gears from followers to leaders. His first point is couched in these words: "But we, brethren, having been bereft of you for a short while—in person, not in spirit—were all the more eager with great desire to see your face" (v. 17). The Greek term translated *bereft* is the word from which we get our word *orphaned.* The prefix on the original Greek term in this verse intensifies it so that it literally means "to be torn away from." Perhaps a better translation of this word would be *kidnapped.* When Paul left the Thessalonians, he felt kidnapped from them. It was a difficult experience for him. But through it all he maintained three positive attitudes.

1. **An Eager Expectation in Spite of Separation.** Paul eagerly looked forward to the day when he would be rejoined with his Thessalonian friends (v. 17).

2. **A Constant Pursuit amidst Satanic Opposition.** Paul tried to rejoin his Thessalonian followers, but his attempts were "thwarted" by Satan (v. 18). The Greek word used here is *egkóptō,* which means, "to cut in on." It was often used to refer to a runner who cut in on the stride of another runner during a race. Satan continually hindered Paul's efforts to reunite with these brothers and sisters. Today, Satan is still carrying out the same opposing tactics among Christians in some of the more significant areas of their walk with God. Thus, we should never ignore the spiritual warfare in which we are engaged (Eph. 6:10-18). Like Paul, we should strive to work against satanic opposition at every turn, realizing that "greater is He who is in [us] than he who is in the world" (1 John 4:4b). On the other hand, we should not attribute all of our problems and struggles to the work of demons (cf. James 1:13-15, where it is said that we alone bear the responsibility for our sins). We need to exercise common sense and spiritual discernment in this critical area.

3. **A Joyful Hope Undiminished by Problems.** This final responsive attitude is communicated in these words: "For who is our hope or joy or crown of exultation? Is it not even you, in the presence of our Lord Jesus at His coming? For you are our glory and joy" (vv. 19-20). Regardless of

the problems Paul encountered, he found great joy in the Thessalonians. They were worth all the pain he experienced. He could rejoice and find an inner joy in the fact that one day he would rejoin them when Christ returns for His own. On this wonderful event, he could hang his hope. *A Personal Observation:* When we become so intense in fighting our battles that we become grim, we lose three things. One is our hope. As we come to believe that we will never make it through the struggle, we begin to feel defeated. We also lose our hunger for God's Word. As our joy decreases, our desire to read, study, and believe His truth diminishes. In the midst of all this, we also lose our sense of humor. We begin to take ourselves too seriously and fail to take God seriously enough. Thus, it is imperative that we face our struggles with a *joyful hope* that no person or thing can take away from us.

IV. Hearing and Doing.

What we have just studied together is great truth. But if we walk away from it without taking the necessary steps to apply it in our own lives, then it has not benefited us at all. So let's review each key truth that we have covered in this lesson, and let's attach to each a corresponding step of action.

A. An attitude of gratitude can be developed by welcoming God's Word. That's what we have heard, but what should we do in response? *We should welcome the truth we hear.*

B. A commitment to contentment will be strengthened by accepting God's will. Our response? *We need to accept the path we walk*—indeed, that's the key to contentment.

C. A happiness amidst heaviness must be cultivated by affirming God's people. What should we do to begin fleshing this out? *We should affirm the people we love.* Unfortunately, it is often easier for us to encourage strangers than our own loved ones. So if we begin by affirming those who are closest to us, it should become easier to edify anyone else who crosses our path.

18

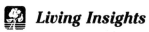 *Living Insights*

Study One ▬▬▬▬▬▬▬▬▬▬▬▬▬▬▬▬▬▬▬▬▬▬▬▬▬▬▬

Nothing can be overlooked by a careful student of the Scriptures. Often times the real meaning of a passage is found through looking at little things—like prepositions, conjunctions, and pronouns.

* Make a copy of this chart in your notebook. In the left column, write in all the pronouns that appear in 1 Thessalonians 2:13-20. Record the reference for each pronoun (we, they, us, them, you, etc.). Then write down the name to which the pronoun refers.

1 Thessalonians 2:13-20 ... Pronouns		
Passage	Pronouns	Person Identified

 Living Insights

Study Two ▬▬▬▬▬▬▬▬▬▬▬▬▬▬▬▬▬▬▬▬▬▬▬▬▬▬▬

This message was filled with many practical applications. Rather than trying to cover them all, let's zero in on one particular aspect ... *affirmation.*

* *We should affirm the people we love.* That was our final statement of application. Do you apply it in your life? What have you done in the last week to affirm those you love? What can you do in the coming week to continue to affirm those people? Write down their names; then put a suggestion next to each name that you'll act upon in the next few days. Watch out, though ... affirmation is contagious!

When Your Comfort Zone
Gets the Squeeze
1 Thessalonians 3:1-8

In our comfort-at-any-cost society, things like affliction, pain, persecution, hardship, and other forms of suffering are viewed as enemies. Many of us who are Christians are frequently surprised, even angered, when we have to endure such difficulties. Unlike the message conveyed by Isaac Watts in his hymn "Am I a Soldier of the Cross?" numerous believers hope to be "carried to the skies on flowery beds of ease." But that is an unrealistic and unbiblical expectation. Repeatedly throughout Scripture we are informed that there is no escape from life's brutal blows. We are also told that we should not view all of them as unfair attacks against us. Indeed, our all-good Lord has included suffering in His plan for each one of us. On the road to glory there must be some barriers to confront and some mountains to scale. Whether we like it or not, the path to the crown is by way of the cross we must bear (Mark 8:34). The section of 1 Thessalonians that we are going to zero in on here will help us to better understand our sufferings and teach us how God wants us to respond to them.

I. To set the record straight . . .

Whenever we pass through a time of real struggle and pain, we usually find ourselves experiencing tension between acceptance and resistance. On one side of the coin, we place our hands in God's sovereign and loving care, realizing that He never makes mistakes. We know that there is a good purpose for everything He allows to pierce our lives (cf. Rom. 8:28). On the flip side, however, we tend to fight against the intrusion of suffering, vowing never to give up the hope that we can endure, even overcome, the parasite that is draining our life from us. Usually we find ourselves responding on both sides; we plead for God to exercise mercy and healing, while trying to rest in His loving control. And through it all, we often ask, Does any of this have to happen at all? Can't suffering and the resultant tension be avoided altogether? Scripture plainly answers no. The biblical response is that suffering is both inevitable and essential. Let's briefly consider just a few of the many passages that touch on these points.

A. Suffering is inevitable. Since sin first entered the world through the disobedience of Adam and Eve (Gen. 3), suffering has been an inescapable part of life. This does not imply that all suffering is a result of a person's own sin. It does imply that much suffering flows from the fact that sin has entered the human race. Indeed, suffering is one thing that we all have in common. Not even Christians are exempt from experiencing the pangs of suffering. Let's look at three passages that make this clear.

20

1. **Philippians 1:29.** The text reads, "For to you it has been granted for Christ's sake, not only to believe in Him, but also to suffer for His sake." This passage refutes the faulty notion that all suffering is the result of personal sin. On the contrary, we may experience hardship for doing what is right, for carrying out God's desired will (cf. Matt. 26:36-27:50; Acts 5:12-42, 7:54-8:3). As Christians, we have been called to suffer in Christ's behalf.
2. **2 Corinthians 4:8-10.** Here we learn that part of the Christian life includes affliction, perplexity, persecution, and near-knockout blows. Why? So that the "life of Jesus . . . may be manifested in our body."
3. **1 Peter 4:12-16.** These verses teach us not to be surprised when affliction comes upon us. In fact, if we are suffering because we are Christians, then we should "keep on rejoicing," realizing that we are "blessed, because the Spirit of glory and of God rests" upon us. Our difficult, painful times can be evidence that we are being obedient to Christ and His commands. And since we live in a world where there are many people who are still in rebellion against God, it should not surprise us when we are victimized by them simply because we are citizens of God's everlasting kingdom.

B. Pain is essential. Even though we want our comfort zone free from pain, God will often invade and squeeze it for our own good. In fact, suffering is essential to our maturing process in Christ. Let's look at two passages that verify this.

1. **Psalm 119:67, 71, 75.** Many times God will use the tool of affliction for the purpose of instructing us more fully in His way and training us to follow Him more completely. It's difficult when God must *make* us to "lie down in green pastures" (Ps. 23:2a), but many times there is no better way for Him to gain our attention.
2. **Ecclesiastes 7:13-14.** Another purpose for adversity is evaluation. Suffering should cause us to take a scrutinizing look at ourselves as we really are. That's the idea tied up in the use of the Hebrew word translated *consider*. Though a self-evaluation will not guarantee what route our future will take, it will help us to understand where we have been and what improvements we can make.

II. Take the Thessalonians, for example . . .

Building on the foundation we have laid above, let's consider the Thessalonians' example of suffering portrayed in 1 Thessalonians 3:1-8.

21

A. Paul's Relational Concern (vv. 1-2, 5). When Paul
ministered among the Thessalonians, he did so "amid much
opposition" (2:2). And when he was torn away from their
presence (2:17), a storm of suffering fell upon the Thessalonians
whom he had established in the faith (2:14). As a consequence,
Paul was genuinely concerned about how these new Christians
were doing through all of this. So he sent Timothy to "strengthen
and encourage" them in their faith (3:2). The Greek term
rendered *strengthen* means "to shore up, to buttress." Timothy
was sent to enable the Thessalonians to stand strong against the
onslaught of persecution. The Greek word for *encourage* is often
translated *comfort*. It conveys the idea of standing alongside
another person in order to put courage into them. Paul sent
Timothy to strengthen and reassure the Thessalonians *in their
faith*. His goal was not to exhort them to gut it out by the sheer
exertion of willpower. Instead, his objective was to edify them
in the fact that God would see them though this—indeed, that
since He was accomplishing a mighty work in them, they were
experiencing the attacks of the enemy. So Paul was calling on
them to stand firm in God's all-sufficient power. For good reason,
Paul was concerned that they would yield to their suffering. He
knew that such would be Satan's goal and that if they succumbed,
his work among them would have been in vain (3:5). Like Paul,
it would be wise for us to follow up on our concerns for the
spiritual condition of other believers. All of us are in a spiritual
warfare, and we cannot be effective in our fight without uniting
and helping each other (Eph. 6:10-20).

B. The Theological Perspective (vv. 3-4). Paul sent Timothy
on his mission so that none of the Thessalonian believers would
be "disturbed by these afflictions." Paul believed that *affliction
need not unsettle God's people.* Why could he maintain this
belief? Because he knew, as did the Thessalonians, that Christians are "destined" for suffering and that they have been
forewarned that suffering will come (vv. 3-4). God's training
program for His children includes hardship and struggle. He
knows that difficulties can smooth out our rough edges as we
travel the road toward holy perfection in Christ (James 1:2-4).
So He destines us for them. But He doesn't just spring them on
us. He warns us in advance so that we won't be scandalized and
taken off guard by them. Instead, we can prepare ourselves to
stand firm through them.

C. The Thessalonians' Personal Responses (vv. 6-8). When
Christians lose their theological moorings and falter in the face
of adversity, three damaging responses generally occur. First,
they harbor resentment toward a former authority figure;

second, they isolate themselves from Christian friends; and finally, they begin to doubt and grow indifferent toward the biblical instruction they used to embrace. The Thessalonian Christians managed to withstand falling prey to all three responses. Paul tells us how they did it.

1. **They refused to blame a former authority for their sufferings** (v. 6). They did not falter in their "faith and love," and they continued to "think kindly" of Paul and his companions.

2. **They desired to maintain close ties with Paul and his associates in ministry** (v. 6). They longed to see Paul and Timothy as much as Paul and Timothy wanted to get together with the Thessalonians.

3. **They maintained a firm commitment to spiritual truth** (vv. 7-8). Paul put it this way: "For this reason, brethren, in all our distress and affliction we were comforted about you through your faith." The Thessalonians did not doubt or grow indifferent to the truth they had received from Paul. Instead, they maintained their convictions and found strength in them, which helped to see them through. Because these new believers were able to endure their trials, Paul and his companions could "really live"—that is, they could be encouraged through their own struggles.

III. Now that we understand . . .

No one enjoys going through tough times. But now that we understand some of what God's Word says about them, let's commit ourselves to embrace and recall these biblical truths.

A. Having our comfort zone invaded is essential . . . not unfair.

B. Suffering hardship as soldiers in battle is expected . . . not unusual. We need to continually keep before us the fact that there's a war going on, and we're right in the middle of it! Therefore, we must hold fast to the truth and consider our sufferings to be relatively unimportant in comparison to our promoting of divine truth.

📖 *Living Insights*

Study One ━━━━━━━━━━━━━━━━━━━━━━━━━━━━━━

The Christian will never have any pain or suffering. Isn't that a great thought? It sure is great, but it's also one other thing . . . WRONG!!

- Our study began with some of the many verses in Scripture that deal with pain. Let's go back over them for our own personal study. As you read each reference, translate your thoughts into some observations, principles, applications, or whatever is most appropriate from the text. (Extra credit: If you finish up with these references and want more, find your own list of texts that refer to suffering and continue the same process!)

Scriptures That Speak on Suffering	
Passages	Principles on Pain
Philippians 1:29	
2 Corinthians 4:8-10	
1 Peter 4:12-16	
Psalm 119:67, 71, 75	
Ecclesiastes 7:13-14	
1 Thessalonians 3:1-8	

📖 *Living Insights*

Study Two ━━━━━━━━━━━━━━━━━━━━━━━━━━━━━━

Ask yourself a very practical question: How can the Scriptures help you during times of pain and suffering? Yet even before you can address that question, you must ensure the fact that the Scriptures are *available* to you.

- One way to keep the Scriptures available to you is to memorize them. Look back over the six references given in study one. Choose one of your favorite verses and begin committing it to memory. Read the passage aloud ten or twelve times. Write it out on a three-by-five-inch index card and keep it with you in the car, at the office, in the kitchen, or wherever. Just keep saying it over and over. Soon you'll discover it to be part of your memory!

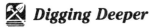 *Digging Deeper*

Two issues were raised in this lesson that deserve further probing. One is the whole subject of *suffering*. Many questions are often raised on this subject by both Christians and non-Christians alike. What is the origin of suffering? Why does God allow it to persist? Why do Christians sometimes suffer more than non-Christians? Will there ever be an end to suffering? If so, when? How does God want His people to handle it in the meantime? What help does God give His own through their suffering? How can we help others through their experiences of adversity? How can the very existence of suffering be reconciled with the existence of an all-good, all-powerful God? Although we have already touched on some of these questions, Scripture gives us a great deal more than we were able to examine here. The second issue involves the subject of *spiritual warfare with demonic forces.* Too often, Christians ignore the reality of demons, or they carry demonic influence to a ridiculous extreme, or they even carelessly dabble in demonic activities. Any one of these responses can lead believers to spiritual ineffectiveness and affliction. We need to realize that we are in a spiritual war! Therefore, we should learn all that we can about it so that we can effectively engage in it. Several sources that address the issues of suffering and spiritual conflict are compiled below. If you would like to dig deeper into these crucial areas and examine them from a scriptural perspective, then we would encourage you to begin with these materials.

- **References on Suffering.**

Baker, Don. *Pain's Hidden Purpose: Finding Perspective in the Midst of Suffering.* Portland: Multnomah Press, 1984.

Bayly, Joseph. *The Last Thing We Talk About.* Revised and enlarged edition. Elgin: David C. Cook Publishing Co., 1973.

Geisler, Norman L. *The Roots of Evil.* Grand Rapids: Zondervan Publishing House; Richardson: Probe Ministries International, 1978.

Lewis, C. S. *A Grief Observed.* New York: The Seabury Press, 1961.

Lewis, C. S. *The Problem of Pain.* New York: Macmillan Publishing Co., Inc., 1962.

Swindoll, Chuck. *For Those Who Hurt.* Portland: Multnomah Press, 1977.

Wiersbe, Warren W. *Why Us? When Bad Things Happen to God's People.* Old Tappan: Fleming H. Revell Co., 1984.

Yancey, Philip. *Helping the Hurting.* Portland: Multnomah Press, 1984.

Yancey, Philip. *Where Is God When It Hurts?* Grand Rapids: Zondervan Publishing House; Wheaton: Campus Life Books, 1977.

- **References on Spiritual Warfare.**
Barnhouse, Donald Grey. *The Invisible War.* Grand Rapids: Zondervan Publishing House, 1965.

Bubeck, Mark I. *Overcoming the Adversary.* Chicago: Moody Press, 1984.

Green, Michael. *I Believe in Satan's Downfall.* Grand Rapids: Wm. B. Eerdman's Publishing Co., 1981.

Lewis, C. S. *The Screwtape Letters.* New York: Macmillan Publishing Co., 1977.

Pentecost, John Dwight. *Your Adversary the Devil.* Grand Rapids: Zondervan Publishing House, 1969.

Swindoll, Charles R. *Demonism.* Portland: Multnomah Press, 1981.

Unger, Merrill F. *Demons in the World Today.* Wheaton: Tyndale House Publishers, Inc., 1971.

What Does It Mean to "Really Live"?

1 Thessalonians 3:9-13

We are bombarded with propaganda on "the good life." Numerous appeals, some subtle and others bold, invite us to buy into a philosophy of life that will make us happy. Usually these appeals are hedonistic or materialistic to the core . . . each one promising us things that will *really* bring us satisfaction. But none of them ever fulfill their promises in any lasting way. Why? Because nothing that is external and temporal is capable of meeting our deepest internal needs. The Apostle Paul realized this truth. He also knew that the so-called good life needed to be replaced with the *real life*. The former provides us with only fantasies and fakes, while the latter brings to us an abundant and fulfilling relationship with the all-good God. Would *you* like to taste the real life? Then read on, and open yourself up to apply what you discover.

I. Left to ourselves, we substitute.

When we fail to consult God about what it means to really live, we come up with substitutes for the real life. King Solomon, in his journal titled Ecclesiastes, referred to these replacements as "devices" (7:29b). The root term of the Hebrew word means "to think through a plan, to arrange clever and imaginative ideas." When we turn from God's way and create our own, we replace the real with the fake, the authentic with the artificial, the means to satisfaction with the means to emptiness. Here are some of the specific substitutes we have devised.

A. Mentally, we substitute knowledge for wisdom.
Wisdom is much more than simply memorizing data. Yet so many of us spend our time acquiring information, while we live as fools.

B. Emotionally, we substitute feelings for facts. Often we opt for pleasure today while ignoring the pain it will bring tomorrow. We choose comfort rather than seriously considering what the consequences will be.

C. Spiritually, we substitute a temporal perspective for an eternal one. We work on the horizontal and forget the vertical. We often live for the present with no eye toward eternity.

II. Listening to God, we change.

How can we *really* live? How can we experience real living—the only avenue to a truly satisfying life regardless of the external circumstances? In 1 Thessalonians 3:9-13, Paul answers this question by giving us a grasp on reality rather than fantasy. He takes us away from "the good life" and transports us into four elements that comprise the real life.

27

A. Joyful in Gratitude (v. 9). Paul expressed his gratefulness to the Thessalonians for all the joy they brought to him. Their friendship and loyalty gave Paul a deep sense of happiness, even though he was going through rough times (cf. 2:17-18, 3:7). He did not let his own circumstances dictate what his attitude toward life would be. Instead, he counted the blessings God had granted him through his association with the Thessalonians (cf. Ps. 103:1-2). As a result, he faced life with a smile rather than a frown.

B. Earnest in Prayer (v. 10). Paul and his fellow workers earnestly prayed "night and day" for the Thessalonian believers. They were fervent and consistent in their petitions to God for these Christians. They were also specific in their prayers. One request they regularly made to the Lord was that they be given the opportunity to see the Thessalonians again. Paul desired that God would override Satan's successes at keeping him from reuniting with his Thessalonian friends. The second request was that Paul and his ministerial workers would have the opportunity to complete what was lacking in the faith of the Thessalonians. In other biblical contexts, the Greek term rendered *complete* carries the idea "to restore a fellow Christian who has wandered" (cf. Gal. 6:1). In other ancient Greek literature, the word is used to describe such things as the setting of a broken bone, the outfitting of a fleet of ships for battle, the equipping of an army, and the mending of torn nets. The word is always used in a constructive way to communicate that help and assistance are needed. Thus, Paul was praying that he and his fellow workers would be given the opportunity to strengthen and deepen the faith of the Thessalonians. *A Personal Challenge:* If you're not already, then begin to get serious about prayer. Start your day with prayer. Permeate your day with prayer. Even end your day with prayer. You don't have to pray hours upon hours, but take at least a few minutes at a time to turn your eyes toward heaven and commune with the living God. Turn your day and situation over to Him. Intercede in behalf of others for their physical, emotional, intellectual, and spiritual needs. None of the time you spend in prayer will ever be wasted.

C. Abounding in Love (vv. 11-12). In these verses we discover the third element in real living: "Now may our God and Father Himself and Jesus our Lord direct our way to you; and may the Lord cause you to increase and abound in love for one another, and for all men, just as we also do for you." Paul wanted the Thessalonians to know that there was a connecting link between the Lord and their love for others. Only the God who *is* love (1 John 4:8) could cause an unselfish love to increase in the lives of the Thessalonian Christians. And notice that their love was to overflow toward one another and "all men"—Christians and non-Christians alike. Indeed, the Greek preposition translated *for* in verse 12 conveys the idea of getting down deep into something. Paul desired that the Lord would cause the Thessalonians to reach deeply with their love into the lives of those within and without their midst. Their love was to be as boundless as the love Paul, Timothy, and Silas had for them. What kind of love were they to express? We could think of it in relation to the letters that spell the word *love*.

1. **L — Listen.** We respect and accept people enough to graciously hear what they have to say.
2. **O — Overlook.** We are quick to pass over and forgive the minor, unpleasant flaws in others.
3. **V — Value.** We demonstrate toward others a sense of respect and honor that clearly overshadows whatever critical comments we may find necessary to make.
4. **E — Express.** Love is demonstrative! We don't just feel love or say loving things, but we manifest our love by doing what is in the best interest of others.

When this kind of love is exercised, both the lover and the loved experience real living.

D. Established in Holiness (v. 13). The result of joyful gratitude, earnest prayer, and abounding love is a life characterized by holiness. Paul says that we are to do these things "so that He may establish your hearts unblamable in holiness before our God and Father at the coming of our Lord Jesus with all His saints." Our standard for purity comes not from human beings but from God. That's why the verse reads that the Thessalonians would be established in holiness *before God*. The Apostle Peter made the same point in these words: "Like the Holy One who called you, be holy yourselves also in all your behavior; because it is written, 'You shall be holy, for I am holy' " (1 Pet. 1:15-16). How long are we to strive in God's power for this standard of holiness? Until that wonderful day when we will finally be with Christ (1 Thess. 3:13). For at that time, "we shall be like Him" (1 John 3:2b), and therefore, we will *be* holy just as He is holy. Then our striving and struggle will be over; we will have achieved by God's enabling grace a life free from sin and pure as untrodden snow. What a perfect end for real living!

III. Learning from this, we grow.

Now that we know what real living is, let's replace our substitutes with the real thing. Let's summarize the steps we need to take in this way:

A. Mentally, let's grow wiser. Let's commit ourselves to applying the knowledge we already have rather than simply acquiring more facts.

B. Emotionally, let's grow stronger. Our decisions should be based on the facts that we know rather than just on our feelings.

C. Spiritually, let's grow purer. We should strive to live holy lives by pleasing God rather than man.

Living Insights

Study One

Joy, prayer, love, and holiness . . . when these four areas begin to come together in our lives, we begin to enter into REAL living.

- Copy the following charts into your notebook. Since these four topics lead to real living, let's do a study of one, two, or perhaps all four. Use your Bible concordance to research references in the Word where these terms occur. After you do this, write one or two summary statements for each topic you research.

Joyful in Gratitude	
Texts	Thoughts

Earnest in Prayer	
Texts	Thoughts

Abounding in Love	
Texts	Thoughts

Established in Holiness	
Texts	Thoughts

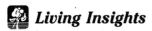 *Living Insights*

Do you know what it means to "really live"? Have you personally experienced it? Let's spend some of our "Living Insights" time reflecting on that penetrating thought.

- Copy this chart onto a blank page in your notebook. Think through each heading in terms of *your life.* Be specific by giving illustrations and incidents from your own experience.

What Does It Mean to "Really Live"?
"Really Living"—What It *Doesn't* Mean:
"Really Living"—What It Means *to Me:*
Personal Life Experiences Which Illustrate the Above:

◣ Digging Deeper

It's one thing to exhort Christians to pray and quite another to teach them to pray. Numerous prayer methods have been offered by well-meaning authors and speakers, many of which are more extravagant and man-centered than realistic and God-centered. To top it off, many available sources are imbalanced. They may provide great-sounding practices with little biblical justification. Or they may present a fine theology of prayer but omit the how-tos of working it out in daily life. Furthermore, far too many sources on prayer do not give biblically sound answers to some of the tough questions: Why should we pray when God knows what we are going to ask Him before we pray? How can prayer change things if God has predetermined all that has occurred and will ever occur? Why does God seem to fail to answer our requests when we firmly believe that our prayers are in line with His will? Why doesn't God always give us the desires of our heart? What we need are some materials that accurately and practically present the scriptural teaching on prayer. Below you will find a list of some of the better Christian books on this important topic. If you would like to probe further into the depths of this essential activity of the Christian life, then you should take the time to work through at least some of these sources. By the way, not all of these materials are for adults. You will find one book for children and another for teenagers. These will help you to introduce nonadults to prayer.

- **References for Further Study.**

   Baughen, Michael. *Breaking the Prayer Barrier: Getting Through to God.* Foreword by James I. Packer. Wheaton: Harold Shaw Publishers, 1981.

   Bounds, Edward McKendree. *Power Through Prayer.* Grand Rapids: Zondervan Publishing House, 1965.

   Hinten, Marvin. *God Is Not a Vending Machine . . . So Why Do We Pray Like He Is?* Grand Rapids: Zondervan Publishing House, 1983.

   Knowles, Andrew. *Discovering Prayer.* A Lion Manual. Belleville: Lion Publishing Corporation, 1985. Designed specifically for teenagers.

   Mitchell, Curtis C. *Praying Jesus' Way: A New Approach to Personal Prayer.* Foreword by Joyce Landorf. Old Tappan: Fleming H. Revell Co., 1977.

   Nystrom, Carolyn. *What Is Prayer?* Illustrated by Wayne A. Hanna. Children's Bible Basics series. Chicago: Moody Press, 1981. An excellent beginner for young children (two to six years old).

   Ogilvie, Lloyd John. *Praying with Power.* Ventura: Regal Books, 1983.

   Sproul, R. C. *Effective Prayer.* Wheaton: Tyndale House Publishers, Inc., 1984.

   Swindoll, Charles R. *Prayer.* Waco: Word Books, 1984.

Straight Talk about Moral Purity
1 Thessalonians 4:1-8

One of the most telltale signs of a deteriorating society is its loss of moral integrity. When this foundational stone begins to crack and erode away, the effect is nothing short of disastrous. Since its inception, Christianity has stood against moral decline by upholding personal holiness. Throughout church history, Christians have remained committed to purity in spite of the ever-present currents of popular opinion and lax moral philosophies that have encouraged them to compromise their stand. A major reason for Christians to maintain such an unbending position is the clear instruction found in God's Word concerning this area. First Thessalonians 4:1-8 stands out in Scripture as one of the more direct passages on moral purity. So, since God has chosen to talk so candidly about this subject, let's decide right now to hear His counsel with our defenses down and our wills geared for submission to Him. With this approach, we can bring glory to God and experience His superabundant goodness in our lives.

I. The Fog: A Brief Analysis of Today's Moral Scene
(Habakkuk 1, Jeremiah 6).
It's easy for many of us to think that the moral decline of our day is relatively new in human history. But that's simply not true. Repeatedly, the Old Testament writers told of incidents, cultures, even eras, that were scarred by various kinds of immorality. Two of these authors served as prophets during the days prior to Judah's fall under the Babylonian invasion (586 B.C.). What they recorded about ancient Judah's moral condition aptly describes the fog of immorality that has clouded our day.

A. The Scream of Habakkuk.
When Habakkuk surveyed Judah's landscape, he saw a people deserving of God's righteous judgment yet desperately in need of His merciful salvation. This ancient prophet described his country as violent (Hab. 1:2b). The land was full of *iniquity*—lying, vanity, and idolatry—and *wickedness*—oppression, robbery, and assault (v. 3a). Strife and contention constantly arose among the people (v. 3b). Indeed, they ignored the law and perverted justice (v. 4). Sound familiar? It's no wonder that Habakkuk screamed out at God to intervene in the fog and put a halt to the moral pollution that had permeated Judah.

B. The Sobs of Jeremiah.
Like Habakkuk, Jeremiah lived and prophesied in Judah during its final stage of political, moral, and religious collapse. And even though he witnessed many of the same immoralities that Habakkuk had observed, it brought him to tears instead of shouts of outrage. Notice some of the

33

observations that he made about the Judeans. He said that they had closed their ears to God's revealed Word—indeed, " 'the word of the Lord [had] become a reproach to them; they [had] no delight in it' " (Jer. 6:10). They were all " 'greedy for gain,' " and the religious leaders were no longer protectors of the truth but were proclaimers of lies (v. 13). In fact, the religious officials had lost their desire to be ministers of true forgiveness and reconciliation. Instead, they were telling people that everything was all right when nothing could have been further from the truth (v. 14). To top it all off, these religious leaders were not even ashamed about the pollution they were perpetuating. " 'They did not even know how to blush' " (v. 15). Sin no longer shocked them. They had grown so accustomed to living in a moral fog that their faces failed to turn red when they encountered impurity. That's an unmistakable, telltale sign of a lack of holiness.

II. The Truth: God's Timeless Counsel for Christians (1 Thessalonians 4:1-8).

Since impurity is an enemy all human beings must face, God doesn't mince words when He addresses the subject. He speaks directly, seriously, and clearly. One such instance is lodged in the fourth chapter of 1 Thessalonians. There the Lord of holiness pierces through the moral fog with the penetrating light of divine truth. He conveys three basic directives that are imperative for us to heed if we are to obey God's command to be holy.

   A. In your walk, excel still more (vv. 1-2). We are not to be lazy or passive in our Christian lives. Instead, we are exhorted to actively pursue personal obedience to the divine commands given in Scripture. This means that we must commit ourselves to submit rather than ignore or revolt against God's standard of holiness (cf. Rom. 6:16-18, 1 Pet. 1:13-16). It also involves our commitment to diligently work through a process that is sometimes difficult and painful, yet fruitful and rewarding (cf. Heb. 12:1-3, James 1:2-4).

   B. In your morals, abstain from sexual immorality (vv. 3-6). If we are going to excel toward the goal of holiness, then we need to get a grip on dealing with sexual lusts. Verse 3 makes it quite plain: "For this is the will of God, your sanctification; that is, that you abstain from sexual immorality." Part of God's will for Christians is that they have no sexual relationships outside the bounds of marriage. This means that bigamy, polygamy, homosexuality, sodomy, prostitution . . . all forms of premarital, extramarital, and nonmonogamous marital sex . . . are wrong. Such relationships are not outlawed because they are unwise, indiscreet, dangerous, unpopular, excessive, or unpleasing. Rather, God forbids them because they violate His holy nature and His holy will for His people. Abstaining from sexual immorality includes the knowledge of how to possess our own vessels in "sanctification and honor" (v. 4). That is, we need to know how to control our own bodies and sexual drives in a pure and upright way. We are not to lose control of ourselves and act "in lustful passion, like the Gentiles who do not know God" (v. 5).

Some Modern Applications

Let's bring this up-to-date for a moment. There are films, television programs, and magazines that weaken us morally because they beckon us toward an immoral lifestyle. Certain conversations carried on by certain people have the same detrimental effect. Specific types of parties, places, and seductive pastimes have a lure toward impurity that we should avoid, regardless of the pressures to attend. We are foolish to think that we can play around with these things without getting hurt. *We must stop tantalizing ourselves with sin!* Our abstinence and avoidance will be for our own good and God's splendid glory.

And just in case someone might think that nothing is wrong with immorality as long as it is only carried out in one's family, God has added these words: "that no man transgress and defraud his brother in the matter because the Lord is the avenger in all these things" (v. 6a). Incestuous practices with family members, such as one's in-laws, parents, stepparents, or children, are labeled as immoral (cf. 1 Cor. 5:1). God will not allow wrongdoing—even on the family level—to go unpunished. He will avenge the injustice. And often, He will not wait until the final judgment day to right a wrong; many wrongdoers—including Christians—will bear the brunt of divine chastisement during their own lifetime (for example, see 1 Cor. 11:20-22, 27-34; Heb. 12:5-13).

C. In your reasoning, remember why God called you (vv. 7-8). We who are Christians should not traffic in immorality, because "God has not called us for the purpose of impurity, but in [the sphere of] sanctification." In other words, when God saved us, it was so that we might begin to grow up spiritually. He wants us to progressively move out of the fog of impurity and into the bright light of holiness (cf. 1 John 1:5-7). Our Lord

35

never intended to give us everlasting life so that we could continue to live as if we were still headed toward everlasting death. Yet many of us are living this way. And when we remain engaged in an immoral lifestyle, we are "not rejecting man but the God who gives His Holy Spirit" to us (v. 8). That's serious business!

III. The Choice: A Decision Only You Can Make.

There are only two options to choose from: to live horizontally in the weakness of the flesh, or to live vertically in the power of the Spirit. Both are diametrically opposed to each other, and both have certain consequences. You must decide which set of consequences you want to live with and die with. Consider them carefully. You must choose one or the other; you cannot straddle the fence that separates them (cf. Matt. 6:24).

A. If you choose to operate horizontally . . .

1. . . . you will drift in a fog of moral uncertainty and decay. You will end up playing religious games while your real life becomes increasingly polluted by the moral impurity and general godlessness surrounding you.

2. . . . your disobedience will result in increasing guilt and grief. God will not permit His children to traffic in sin without their experiencing the pain and anguish that eventually accompanies it. And this He does "for our good, that we may share in His holiness" (Heb. 12:10b).

B. If you choose to operate vertically . . .

1. . . . you will honor the God of moral absolutes. Your submission to the Lord's holy commands will bring Him glory.

2. . . . your obedience will result in greater confidence and habits of holiness. In time, your obedience will increase your strength to say no to sin as you conform more to God's perfect standard of spiritual maturity—holiness.

 *Living Insights*

We learned from Jeremiah that a telltale sign of a lack of holiness is the failure to blush at sin. Because God desires that His people be holy, He talks candidly to the Thessalonians, you, and me about moral purity.

- Let's get a real handle on this passage. One of the best methods of doing this is a technique known as *paraphrasing*. This means that you write out the verses in your own words. Let's try this with 1 Thessalonians 4:1-8. Seek to discover the true meanings of the words as you make your paraphrase. Also, attempt to get behind the words to the feelings and emotions that punctuate this passage. Use this entire exercise to help yourself gain a better understanding of the issue of moral purity.

 Living Insights

We need to perfect a strategy that will help us stay clear of things that appeal to our sensual lusts. Use the thoughts that follow to carefully map out the danger zones in your own personal battle with lust. Be specific in your answers. Then take the steps that are necessary for avoiding those lures that lead you into sin.

- Are there certain forms of media you should avoid?
    Magazines?
    Films?
    Pictures?
    Television?
    Books?

- Are there certain people who prompt lust in your life?
    By their conversation?
    By their lifestyle?
    By their appearance?

- Are there certain activities in your life that stimulate sensuality?
    Parties?
    Places to meet?
    Seductive pastimes?

Behaving Properly toward Outsiders

1 Thessalonians 4:9-12

What is the Christian's responsibility toward non-Christians? Are the saved to conduct their affairs as if unbelievers didn't exist? Or are they to treat outsiders as though they had some kind of contagious plague and thus are in need of being kept at a safe distance? Should Christians try to avoid offending non-Christians by adopting their lifestyle? How should believers behave toward unbelievers? What does God's Word say about this? In this lesson, we are going to find out the answers to these questions. As we do, let's bear in mind certain categories of outsiders who usually cross our paths, such as immediate family members, relatives, neighbors, work associates, fellow classmates, friends, and even casual acquaintances. The answers we discover in Scripture will affect not only our lives but theirs as well.

I. A Necessary Warning and Challenge to All Christians.

All of us who are Christians are engaged in an intense conflict—the war of extremes. This war is waged on a variety of fronts. Let's briefly look at four of them. The first occurs between *faithful evangelism and personal edification.* Either we are zealous for the lost and inclined toward evangelism, almost to the exclusion of personal development through Bible study and prayer, or we are so committed to our spiritual growth that we exercise little to no concern for those who are without Christ. A second battle of extremes occurs between *enthusiastic faith and a healthy trust in God.* On the one hand, we can act with such self-confidence and determination that we run ahead without God's help and make a mess of things. On the other hand, we can be so afraid of risk and the walk of faith that we excuse ourselves from involvement and, as a result, become dull and visionless. Another conflict arises between *the vertical and the horizontal.* The vertical side is often characterized by a preoccupation with prophecy, identifying signs of the end times, and focusing on Christ's imminent return. This occurs to such a degree that we live recklessly and irresponsibly, expecting His return to bail us out of the mess we have created for ourselves. The horizontal side involves ignoring the truths of the vertical so completely that we despair of Christ's return. Consequently, we set about building our own materialistic empire and utopia. A fourth fight between extremes occurs as the result of our need to maintain *relationships with both Christians and non-Christians.* We can become so exclusive and inbred that our whole world revolves around other Christians. This leads to our losing touch with the lost.

Or we can slip into the other extreme, where we choose to avoid contact so thoroughly with fellow Christians and biblical teaching that we end up as "secret service saints" who behave little differently than the non-Christian world.

A. A Caution. Each of these extremes is wrong. God wants us to be not extremist Christians but balanced ones. So, what's the caution? *Guard against extremes!* But beware. Satan will try to break down your defenses against extremism because he is the expert of the unbalanced life. He was not satisfied to be the highest-ranking, angelic servant of God. He wanted to rule as God (Isa. 14:12-14). Then, when the Lord judged him for his sin, he became the most corrupt and devious rebel in God's entire kingdom. Such a sinful extremist will do all he can to get and keep us off balance. So watch out for him and his tricks.

B. Some Clarification. In John 17, Jesus prayed to His Heavenly Father and asked Him to keep His children from extremism—specifically, from the extremes of (1) losing touch with unbelievers because of Christian exclusivism and (2) becoming so worldly that no noticeable Christian distinctives exist. Read carefully these words from Jesus' petition:

> "I do not ask Thee to take them out of the world, but to keep them from the evil one. They are not of the world, even as I am not of the world. Sanctify them in the truth; Thy word is truth. As Thou didst send Me into the world, I also have sent them into the world" (John 17:15-18).

The Lord does not save us so that He can remove us from the world. Rather, He rescues us from the path of destruction, then calls on us to present the only path to life to those travelers who are still going the wrong way. Jesus prayed for our insulation from Satan, not our isolation from the world. We can only be salt and light to a dying world when we involve ourselves *in* it without becoming *like* it.

C. A Challenge. In 1 Corinthians 5, the Apostle Paul applied the essence of Christ's prayer to a situation that had arisen in the Corinthian church. The Corinthian believers had gone to an extreme. They had become so worldly that they condoned an incestuous relationship in their midst—one that would have shocked even the non-Christian world (1 Cor. 5:1). Paul strongly rebuked these believers for not disciplining a Christian who had become sexually intimate with his father's wife (vv. 1-5). Then he backed up his rebuke with these words of clarification:

> I wrote you in my letter not to associate with immoral people; I did not at all mean with the immoral people of this world, or with the covetous and swindlers, or

with idolaters; for then you would have to go out of the world. But actually, I wrote to you not to associate with any so-called brother if he should be an immoral person, or covetous, or an idolater, or a reviler, or a drunkard, or a swindler—not even to eat with such a one (vv. 9-11).

The challenge is clear. First, *Christians need to remain distinctive in and attractive to the world without living like the world.* Second, *Christians need to be tough on their own and, in comparison, easy on non-Christians.* We need to quit expecting non-Christians to behave as Christians should and stop excusing Christians for behaving as non-Christians usually do.

II. Some Balanced Counsel from Early Christians.

Paul, Silvanus, and Timothy (1:1) provide the counsel all Christians should heed for behaving properly toward the unsaved. Their instruction in 1 Thessalonians 4:9-12 is basically twofold.

A. When It Comes to Fellow Christians (vv. 9-10). Their first piece of counsel is basic yet foundational to the unity of the Church and its witness to a watching world. What is it? *That Christians love one another.* Look at what these verses say: "Now as to the love of the brethren, you have no need for anyone to write to you, for you yourselves are taught by God to love one another; for indeed you do practice it toward all the brethren who are in all Macedonia. But we urge you, brethren, to excel still more." The Thessalonian Christians not only knew that they were supposed to love fellow believers, but they made their knowledge come alive in their relationships with other Christians. They were not simply hearers of the truth but were doers as well. And yet, Paul and his co-workers exhorted them to *excel even more at loving other Christians.* The Thessalonians were called to do that which was best for fellow believers to the highest degree attainable. Their love was to be modeled after the sacrificial love Christ manifested toward them when He willingly died on the cross in man's behalf (cf. John 3:16, 13:1, 15:13; Rom. 5:6-8). When Christians display this kind of love toward one another, it attracts the attention of the unsaved. Why? Because non-Christians are used to a love that must be earned. So when they are confronted with unconditional love—a love that accepts others regardless of who they are rather than for what they can achieve—they see something that they want. That desire generally opens a natural door for sharing the good news about Jesus Christ. The Lord was well aware that the exercise of genuine Christian love among His people would have this effect. That's why He instructed His disciples with these

words: " 'A new commandment I give to you, that you love one another, even as I have loved you.... By this all men will know that you are My disciples, if you have love for one another' " (John 13:34-35).

B. When It Comes to Non-Christians (vv. 11-12). A more direct way in which we may behave properly toward unbelievers is laid before us in these verses from 1 Thessalonians. Basically, what is set forth is *lifestyle evangelism.* Let's consider the three key elements listed that comprise this witnessing method as well as its usual result.

    1. Lead a quiet life. There is good reason to believe that many in the Thessalonian church had gone overboard on prophecy—specifically, the imminent return of Jesus Christ. Some among them had quit their jobs and begun spending their time in idle conversation and speculation about this supernatural event. So Paul exhorted them to stop spending an inordinate amount of time living in tomorrow and to start living with a calm, responsible eye on today.

    2. Attend to your own business. The idea in this command is one of personal diligence—working steadily and faithfully at one's own assignment in life (cf. John 21:20-22). The Thessalonians were not to be busybodies, obnoxious, or wearisome about their Christian beliefs. They were to do their share in the ongoing maintenance and development of Thessalonica by attending to their own work.

    3. Work with your hands. The Thessalonian Christians were to earn their own way in the community. They were not to freeload off of one another or non-Christians. Apparently, some of these early believers thought that there was nothing wrong with leading a lazy life and reaping the benefits of other people's hard work. So, in another letter to them, Paul had to reiterate this exhortation to work in much stronger terms (2 Thess. 3:10-15). Few things damage the effective spreading of the gospel more than a Christian who does a job poorly or hardly at all. We who are Christians need to work hard and well. As we do, respect for our labor will eventually create ample opportunities for us to share the faith.

    4. This lifestyle will win you the right to be heard and make you less dependent on others. Of course, there are exceptions to this general consequence. But the main point is this: *A loving, responsible lifestyle will not only benefit other Christians and yourself, but it will also bring to the watching eyes of the lost a magnetic view of the life that could be theirs through Jesus Christ.*

III. Some Practical Advice Regarding Non-Christians.

Keeping in mind the wise counsel we have just considered, let's turn our attention to one more biblical text and draw our final pieces of advice from it. The verses read, "Conduct yourselves with wisdom toward outsiders, making the most of the opportunity. Let your speech always be with grace, seasoned, as it were, with salt, so that you may know how you should respond to each person" (Col. 4:5-6). The instruction presented here regarding Christians' behavior before non-Christians is clear. Let's personalize it for your benefit.

A. **Non-Christians are watching and wondering, so conduct yourselves with wisdom.** Don't let your actions contradict your witness. Be an example of what you believe—even before you share it verbally.

B. **Non-Christians are listening and learning, so speak your words with grace.** No rebukes, put-downs, insults, or suggestions of superiority are needed or wanted when you convey your faith to unbelievers. Let your speech be bathed in God's superabundant grace. When it is, forgiveness and unconditional love, not condemnation and haughty pride, will be its hallmarks.

C. **Non-Christians are individuals and important, so respond to them with dignity and sensitivity.** Every Christian has a different background. Hence, each has varying expectations, abilities, needs, and struggles. The same is true of every non-Christian. As servants of the One who gave His life for every human being, we need to treat each person as a distinct individual who is greatly loved by God.

 Living Insights

Study One

This is such a rich passage of Scripture. It's the kind of text that grows more meaningful with each reading. Let's try a method of study that will be especially helpful with these verses.

- Search around the house and locate as many different versions of the Bible as you can. Read 1 Thessalonians 4:9-12 in each version. It may be a translation or a paraphrase; it doesn't matter. Both will be very helpful in giving you further meaning and depth in this great text. After you've done this, jot down your most significant thoughts on paper.

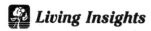 *Living Insights*

After a message on dealing with outsiders, an important question needs to be asked: *Are you an outsider?* If so, are you ready to come in? But if you are already a believer, what are you doing to reach the outsiders around you?

- If you're *without Christ,* take this opportunity to receive Him as your personal Savior. When He died on the cross for sins, He included yours. He offers you the free gift of eternal life. All you need to do is simply trust Him for it. Begin your relationship with Christ . . . now!

- If you *know Christ,* gather your family or roommates together to discuss the impact you're making on the neighborhood. Are there any areas of imbalance? Are you excelling? Remember, those around you are watching and listening. Talk about how you can respond to them with sensitivity.

On That Great Gettin'-Up Morning

1 Thessalonians 4:13-18

For centuries, thoughtless fanatics have littered the path of Christianity—especially those who have earned the label "prophecy freaks." Most of them have been well-intentioned, highly intense souls who have found it almost impossible to retain their equilibrium with the subject of the future. As a consequence, they have left in their wake messes of tragic proportion, the worst of which has been the reactionary fallout. These fanatics have consistently turned scores of people away from the Bible's prophetic message. Instead of sifting through the hype and abuse of God's prophetic program, many people have reacted by discounting and even scoffing at the biblical picture of the future. Christians today need to take a sane and sober reexamination of God's plan for the events yet to come. We will consider a slice from it in this study. And although we will uncover no dates, nor discover every future event spelled out in detail, we will learn enough to help us live more wisely in the here and now while we anxiously await the yet to come.

I. Extremes We Need to Guard Against.

The return of Christ is the most mentioned event in all Scripture. In the New Testament alone, it is referred to over three hundred times. Indeed, the Lord's final recorded words in the Bible concern His imminent return (Rev. 22:20). Unfortunately, this biblical truth has been met with two extreme reactions that we need to avoid.

A. Fanatical Intensity. This reaction characterizes those individuals who go off the deep end concerning prophecy. They often try to set a date when Christ will return, even though He said centuries ago that such predictions were doomed to fail (Matt. 24:36, Acts 1:6-7). These people usually see prophetic significance in every news headline and contemporary event. Their vision is so fixed on Christ's coming and related future events that they are generally irresponsible when it comes to present, earthly matters.

B. Theological Ignorance. The other extreme is to be completely unaware or disinterested in the Savior's imminent return. People who react in this way do not realize or care that the events of history are occurring in accordance with God's infallible timetable. All too often, their lack of heavenly mindedness seriously hinders their evangelistic zeal, personal purity, and exercise of hope in a better life beyond their earthly one. Christians must seek a balance in the area of prophecy. Those who are future minded in a scriptural way are of more present good than those who go to one extreme or the other.

44

II. Truth We Can Count On.

The first step to achieving balance in prophetic matters is to consult the Scriptures. Only there are we provided with the clear, trustworthy revelation of what God desires for us to know about His future plans. First Thessalonians 4:13-18 presents us with some of this material. In fact, these verses were written to bring a balanced perspective to some early Christians who had gone to extremes concerning Christ's return. The passage was also composed to settle the fears of other believers who apparently had been told that deceased Christians would not be resurrected when Christ returned. The bottom line is that this text does not venture into fanatical speculation; rather, it sets forth prophetic truth that we can count on no matter what!

A. Regarding Our Death and Resurrection (vv. 13-14).

Some Christians in Thessalonica had been misinformed "about those who are asleep"—in other words, those Christians who had already died. These deceased believers were with the Lord spiritually (2 Cor. 5:6-8, Phil. 1:23), but their bodies were physically "asleep" in the earth. The Apostle Paul wanted to give these ill-informed believers the data needed to handle their grief over deceased brethren with a sense of *hope*. This would be quite unlike the grief experienced by unbelievers, for many non-Christians believe that there is no life after death; therefore, they have no tomorrow to look forward to . . . no expectation that one day they will be reunited with the ones they deeply miss. Christians, however, need not despair through the intense pain felt because of the death of a Christian loved one. They can have hope in the midst of their sorrow and hurt. On what basis? Look at verse 14: "For if we believe that Jesus died and rose again, even so God will bring with Him those who have fallen asleep in Jesus." Our hope, as Christians, is grounded in the historical fact of Christ's physical death and bodily resurrection from the dead. When individuals put their trust in this Savior, we can rest assured that death will not close the book on their lives. Rather, death for them will eventually result in their resurrection from the grave to everlasting life with Christ. And what effect will this resurrection event have on a Christian's body? Plenty! The decay, disease, and weaknesses that plague our bodies now will be stripped away. Our perishable and mortal bodies will become imperishable and immortal. The things that tear and wear us down will no longer have a grip on us. When Christ returns, He will upgrade all His people to the status of Christlikeness, even in their own bodies (1 Cor. 15:50-55, 1 John 3:2).

B. Regarding Christ's Coming and Others' Joining
(vv. 15-17). In these verses God unveils the specific order of events accompanying Christ's return. Let's examine them in the order they are given, which is also the sequence in which they will occur in human history.

1. **First, Christ will return to earth** (v. 16a). Presently, Jesus is seated at the right hand of God the Father in heaven (Rom. 8:34, Eph. 1:20, Col. 3:1, Heb. 1:3). At the time that has been set by the Father (Acts 1:6-7), Christ will leave His position and "descend from heaven with a shout, with the voice of the archangel, and with the trumpet of God." The dramatic and majestic events accompanying His return will certainly be worthy of the King of kings and Lord of lords.

2. **Second, deceased Christians will rise from their graves** (v. 16b). Exactly how God will reassemble and resurrect these believers is not mentioned. But that He has the power and knowledge to do it is beyond question. After all, anyone who could create the entire universe from nothing (John 1:3) and sustain the whole created order in existence (Col. 1:17) could certainly manage some bodily resurrections.

3. **Third, living Christians will be transported with the resurrected Christians to meet Christ "in the air"** (v. 17a). At this time, the bodies of all living believers will be changed to imperishable and immortal bodies—just like those of the resurrected believers (1 Cor. 15:51-52). Of course, the Rapture will occur "in a moment, in the twinkling of an eye," but the point is that it *will* happen just as God says it will.

4. **Fourth, all the resurrected and raptured Christians will be with Christ forever** (v. 17b). Never will they be able to lose their new life with the Lord. They will be secured in Him forevermore.

C. Regarding Confidence and Comfort (v. 18). The conclusion of this great prophetic passage seems only natural: "Therefore comfort one another with these words." Notice that it does *not* say that these wonderful truths should prompt us to set dates, sell our possessions, and watch for Christ's return from the highest mountain. Nor does it suggest that we should go our merry way without paying any further regard to these future events. Rather, God wants us to take this knowledge and use it to comfort and encourage each other. When we grieve, we need to be encouraged with these truths so that our sorrow will be permeated with hope, not despair. We can find strength in the fact that one day our Lord will call us home to be with Him forever—strength even when we experience mistreatment, wonder whether our evangelistic efforts are worthwhile, or become tired of struggling against temptation.

III. Our Response to Christ's Soon Coming.

How can we prepare for the Lord's imminent return? What is an appropriate response to this assured prophetic event? In Titus 2:11-13 we can find a simple, threefold answer.

A. Make certain that you have personally received the salvation God has provided for you (v. 11). Through Jesus Christ, God has made it possible for all sinners—including you—to be pardoned from their sins. Your pardon has been secured by Christ, who willingly chose to pay for your death sentence by giving up His own life for yours. However, your pardon does not become effective until you accept Christ's payment for your sins. When you do trust in His death, God will grant your pardon and give you everlasting life. Not until you take this step of faith will you ever be able to have a firm hope that will carry you through this life and into the life beyond.

B. Continue to resist a corrupt lifestyle (v. 12a). Don't let Christ's sudden return catch you off guard. Keep on preparing for His coming by constantly fighting against "ungodliness and worldly desires."

C. Live in a sensible, godly manner (vv. 12b-13). Don't fall prey to prophetic fanaticism or ignorance. Instead, mature in a lifestyle that brings God glory and honor in the present, while you anxiously await "the blessed hope and the appearing of the glory of our great God and Savior, Christ Jesus."

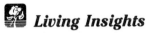 *Living Insights*

Can you imagine the headlines in your local newspapers the day Jesus Christ returns! Many fine writers have attempted to use some "sanctified imagination" in visualizing this scene. Let's return to the biblical account of this event.

- You've been recruited by your local newspaper to write a story on the return of Jesus Christ, as presented in 1 Thessalonians 4:13-18. The first step necessary is to *ask questions*. Make a copy of the following chart to help channel your thinking in this direction. After you ask the questions listed, *supply their answers from the text*. Finally, write up your news story!

1 Thessalonians 4:13-18	
Questions	Answers
Who?	
What?	
Where?	
When?	
Why?	
How?	

Study Two ━━━━━━━━━━━━━━━━━━━━━━━━━━━

Are you ready for the soon coming of Christ? Does that thought bring peace and excitement to your heart? Or does it foster frustration and uneasiness?

- The following chart asks one typical question and one less-asked question. Write down honest answers to both of them. Think through some ways to improve yourself in view of the second question, then close your study by praying for God's help in making those improvements.

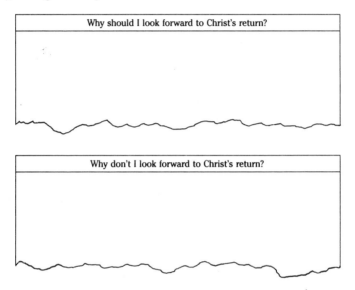

Why should I look forward to Christ's return?

Why don't I look forward to Christ's return?

"... Like a Thief in the Night"

1 Thessalonians 5:1-11

People have an insatiable thirst for knowledge about the future. This explains the public's interest in astrology, horoscopes, mediums, and seers. It also tells us why books on prophecy sell so well, and it explains why half-empty churches can become packed when a sermon is given on end-time events. Among the numerous prophecies recorded in the Bible, few draw more of our attention than those concerning "the day of the Lord." First Thessalonians 5:1-11 presents a succinct overview of this awesome future event. In this lesson we will discover how "the day of the Lord" relates to both non-Christians and Christians.

I. The Subject of Prophecy.

Throughout history, people have been curious about what will occur in the future. Indeed, we seem to have an innate desire to know what is going to happen before it actually does. Why is this so? Because God has placed eternity in our hearts (Eccles. 3:11). We long to understand that which lies beyond us. Of course, this intense desire is not always satisfied. In fact, much about tomorrow is shrouded in mystery . . . left in uncertainty. This usually makes us uncomfortable. We want to know the fine details because we often think that by knowing them, we will be better prepared to face the future. Christ's disciples felt the same way. They were not satisfied with just a general outline of the future. Twice we read that they asked Jesus to fill in the sketch with more detail. The first time, which is recorded in Matthew 24-25, He responded by giving them more specifics. However, the second time, His answer was much different. Just read what happened:

> And so when they had come together, they were asking Him, saying, "Lord, is it at this time You are restoring the kingdom to Israel?" He said to them, "It is not for you to know times or epochs which the Father has fixed by His own authority; but you shall receive power when the Holy Spirit has come upon you; and you shall be My witnesses both in Jerusalem, and in all Judea and Samaria, and even to the remotest part of the earth" (Acts 1:6-8).

Obviously, Jesus thought that the disciples had all the details about the future that they needed. So He turned their attention from the yet-to-come to the here-and-now—specifically, from prophetic date-setting to the tasks of evangelism and missions. We can see from this that there will be some future events that God will inform us about. But that does not mean that He will unveil them in every detail. Some things will remain a mystery to us until we look at them in retrospect.

II. The Day of the Lord (1 Thessalonians 5:1-11).

Among the many prophecies recorded in Scripture, few are more detailed than those regarding "the day of the Lord," and none foretell a more destructive event. Many of the specifics concerning this Great Tribulation period are revealed in Revelation 6-19. The Apostle Paul provides a thumbnail sketch of this prophecy in the fifth chapter of his first letter to the Thessalonians. In the first several verses, he briefly explains how this day will come, what impact it will have on non-Christians, and how it relates to Christians.

A. The Coming of the Day (vv. 1-2). Paul begins with this reminder: "Now as to the times and the epochs, brethren, you have no need of anything to be written to you." Apparently, during Paul's first visit with the Thessalonians, he had spelled out to them many of the biblical details regarding "the day of the Lord." That's why he could say in the next verse, "For you yourselves know full well that the day of the Lord will come just like a thief in the night." These Christians already knew what the coming of that prophetic event would be like. Paul merely had to recall to their attention what they had previously learned. But this was not the case with the future resurrection of deceased Christians and the future rapture of living Christians. Because the Thessalonians had been misinformed about them, he had to set them straight on those events (4:13-18). This suggests that Paul had not yet taught them those truths. Now, in his reminder about "the day of the Lord," Paul says that it will come "like a thief in the night"—that is, it will come unexpectedly and unannounced (cf. Matt. 24:42-44, Luke 12:39-40). This event is quite different from the resurrection and rapture of believers that were described in the former lesson. Those events will be dramatically announced by "the Lord Himself [who] will descend from heaven with a shout, with the voice of the archangel, and with the trumpet of God" (1 Thess. 4:16).

B. Unbelievers and the Day (v. 3). Continuing in 1 Thessalonians 5, Paul writes, "While they are saying, 'Peace and safety!' then destruction will come upon them suddenly like birth pangs upon a woman with child; and they shall not escape" (v. 3). The pronoun changes from *you* and *we* (4:13-5:2) to *they* and *them* indicate that Paul is not including himself or his Christian readers in the day-of-the-Lord prophecy. And for good reason: He did not expect that any Christian living before that terrible period would experience it because God would have already raptured them from the earth (4:15-17). Therefore, only unbelievers will witness the unannounced beginning of this judgment time. Notice also that it will come when non-Christians are saying that all is well with the world. But instead of reaping the benefits of genuine peace, they will suddenly be plunged into a catastrophic period of divine judgment from which there will be no escape.

C. Believers and the Day (vv. 4-11). Again, these verses begin with a change in pronouns. Paul turns away from focusing on unbelievers and directs his remarks in these verses toward Christians.

    1. Don't be sleepy and drunk, but remain alert and sober (vv. 4-8). He starts with these words of contrast: "But you, brethren, are not in darkness, that the day should overtake you like a thief; for you are all sons of light and sons of day. We are not of night nor of darkness; so then let us not sleep as others do, but let us be alert and sober" (vv. 4-6). The lost are either unaware or unmoved by the coming of a great judgment day. Christians, however, have too much information about it to respond in that way. They know that God's wrath will be poured out upon the earth during a seven-year period of judgment called the Great Tribulation (Rev. 6-19). They are also aware that just prior to the beginning of that horrible day, Christ will return for them and literally transport them to a place of safety with Him (1 Thess. 4:15-17, Rev. 3:10). Therefore, Christians are to remain on the lookout. They are not to yawn through life but are to stay alert. And how are they to do this? By putting on the "breastplate of faith and love, and as a helmet, the hope of salvation" (1 Thess. 5:8). In other words, we who are believers are to live as people of the light, not as the unsaved who carry on their existence in the realm of darkness (v. 7). Like well-protected and alert guards, we are called to carry out our Christian responsibilities with the conviction of faith, the selfless ministry of love, and the assurance of our deliverance from divine judgment. When we live this way, we will not fail to be mentally active, spiritually alert, and prophetically aware.

    2. Remember your destination (vv. 9-10). In contrast to non-Christians who are headed for the divine wrath yet to come, Christians have been destined by God to inherit their full salvation when Christ returns for them prior to the Tribulation. What a wonderful source of joy and security! It also gives us believers another reason to remain prepared and alert. We do not want to be caught trafficking in sin when our Savior comes to deliver us. We need to keep our house in order in anticipation of His imminent return. We also need to get the word out to the world that no one has to experience "the day of the Lord." Like us, any person who trusts in Christ as his Deliverer will be rescued from God's wrath during the Great Tribulation and forevermore (cf. Rom. 5:1, 9).

3. **Encourage and edify one another** (v. 11). To the Christian, the prophecies of the Resurrection and Rapture are sources of comfort and joy. Therefore, rather than spend our remaining days finding flaws in one another and trying to tear each other down, we should affirm and strengthen each other with the expectant hope of these events.

III. The Issue of Urgency.

Flowing from this passage are two exhortations—one for Christians and another for non-Christians. Both exhortations carry with them a sense of urgency since no one other than God knows exactly when these prophetic events will occur.

A. **To Believers: Don't be indifferent because tomorrow is secure.** A balanced view of the future should bring us an intense concern to mature in a lifestyle of godliness and to present the good news of salvation to the lost. So if you're a Christian, get to work! There's no time to delay.

B. **To Unbelievers: Don't be fooled because today seems calm.** There's a storm on the horizon. It could break through human history at any moment. So if you're a non-Christian, don't slip into complacency simply because your life may be running smoothly. You will not escape the coming judgment unless you place your life in Christ's hands. Do it now! Don't be caught unprepared and asleep.

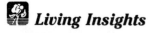 *Living Insights*

The impact of the subject of prophecy cannot be underestimated. Thus, it is crucial for the student of prophecy to carefully examine key prophetical passages. Our current text is one of these.

- Let's break down this passage into smaller elements ... *key words.* After you make a copy of the following chart, read through 1 Thessalonians 5:1-11. Jot down key words in the left column and write the references corresponding to them in the middle column. After you complete these columns, seek to define the terms based on your understanding of the verses or perhaps with the help of a good Bible dictionary. Don't hurry through a study of this nature. Your time will be well rewarded!

"... Like a Thief in the Night"—1 Thessalonians 5:1-11		
Key Words	Verses	Meanings

 Living Insights

"Therefore encourage one another, and build up one another, just as you also are doing" (1 Thess. 5:11). Because of the coming of Christ, we can lift our voices in praise to Him. By doing so, we build up one another. How edifying!

- Let's take God seriously ... let's encourage one another and build up one another. But let's do it in a different manner. Let's *sing* to one another. Music serves such a wonderful purpose in the Body of Christ. It can really lift our spirits. So bring together a group of people and sing praises to your Father! Sing some well-known hymns, some new choruses, or both. Don't be inhibited to speak to "one another in psalms and hymns and spiritual songs" (Eph. 5:19).

 *Digging Deeper*

For centuries, Christians have agreed that there will be a Rapture. But this is where the agreement has stopped. While upholding the certainty of this future event, Christians have disagreed over where to place it in relation to another prophetic occurrence—the Tribulation. Regarding these two events, there have been basically three positions: Pretribulationism (the Rapture precedes the Tribulation); Midtribulationism (the Rapture occurs during the Tribulation); and Posttribulationism (the Rapture marks the end of the Tribulation). If you would like to plunge into the pros and cons of each position in order to decide for yourself which one has the greatest scriptural support, then you would do well to begin with the sources given below. There you will find two lists. The first list sets forth the central biblical passages on the Rapture, and the second mentions several books that explain and evaluate the three major views on this end-time event. We would strongly urge you to do your own study in the biblical texts first. After you have a good grasp on their teaching, then begin to work through the other sources given. Approaching the issue this way will provide you with a firmer foundation from which you can make more informed decisions than you would be able to make otherwise. And remember, Christianity does not stand or fall on one's position on the Rapture and the Tribulation. A disagreement over this issue should not bring about ill-feelings or hostility. This is definitely an intramural debate among Christians that should be carried out in an atmosphere of love and unity, not hate and division.

● **Key Biblical Texts.**

Daniel 9:24-27, Matthew 24-25, Luke 17:20-37, 1 Corinthians 15:20-58, 1 Thessalonians 4:13-5:11, 2 Thessalonians 2:1-12, Revelation 3:10.

● **Significant Christian Books.**

Archer, Gleason L., Jr., et al. *The Rapture: Pre-, Mid-, or Post-Tribulational.* Contemporary Evangelical Perspectives series. Grand Rapids: Zondervan Publishing House, 1984. This book presents Christian thinkers who maintain differing positions on the Rapture and interact with each other over their differences.

Buswell, J. Oliver, Jr. *A Systematic Theology of the Christian Religion.* Vol. II. Grand Rapids: Zondervan Publishing House, 1963. Pages 431-59. Midtribulational.

Gundry, Robert H. *The Church and the Tribulation: A Biblical Examination of Posttribulationism.* Contemporary Evangelical Perspectives series. Grand Rapids: Zondervan Publishing House, 1973. Posttribulational.

Harrison, Norman B. *The End: Rethinking the Revelation.* Minneapolis: Harrison, 1941. Midtribulational.

Ladd, George Eldon. *The Blessed Hope.* Grand Rapids: Wm. B. Eerdmans Publishing Co., 1956. Posttribulational.

Ryrie, Charles C. *What You Should Know about the Rapture.* Chicago: Moody Press, 1981. Pretribulational.

Walvoord, John F. *The Blessed Hope and the Tribulation.* Contemporary Evangelical Perspectives series. Grand Rapids: Zondervan Publishing House, 1976. Pretribulational.

Gifts to Give the Family

1 Thessalonians 5:12-15

Every Christmas season we face the same question: What gifts should I give my family members? For one reason or another, we often have difficulty deciding what to give. However, when it comes to our selecting gifts for fellow members in God's forever family, the Lord has made the decision process quite easy. In fact, He has eliminated it altogether, for He has provided us with a divinely approved gift list in 1 Thessalonians 5:12-22. In this lesson, we will work our way through the first part of the list (vv. 12-15). In the next study, we will turn our attention to the second part of this list (vv. 16-22). As we examine the itemized gifts, let's bear in mind that God's desire is that we give *each* gift to one another. By doing so, we will make life in His family a much more enriching experience.

I. Worthwhile Qualities in Whatever We Give.

When presenting gifts to fellow Christians, we ought to strive to offer gifts that are genuinely worth giving. But how can we discover which gifts are worthwhile? By examining them to see if they possess the following four qualities:

   A. Worthy gifts last. We should give gifts that have a permanency about them. Lasting gifts are quality gifts.

   B. Worthy gifts lift up. Gifts that are really meaningful to family members are those that edify and build up both the giver and the receiver.

   C. Worthy gifts cost. Anyone can give a present that is free or cheap. But when someone gives a gift that requires personal sacrifice to acquire, that makes the present valuable—even priceless.

   D. Worthy gifts glorify God. Whatever gifts we give to another believer should bring a smile of approval to God's face. Gifts that honor and exalt the Lord are the most precious of all.

II. Worthwhile Gifts to Give Away.

Paul mentions four kinds of gifts in 1 Thessalonians 5:12-22: those that are kindly requested (vv. 12-13); those that are urgently needed (vv. 14-15); those that are continually appropriate (vv. 16-20); and that which is occasionally uncertain (vv. 21-22). We want to pause and take a closer look at the first two types of gifts in this lesson. As we do, remember that since these gifts have God's stamp of approval, they possess all the qualities that make them worthwhile to give.

   A. Gifts Kindly Requested (vv. 12-13). There are two in this category. Paul states one as a request and the other as a command.

   1. **Respect those in leadership** (vv. 12-13a). These verses read, "But we request of you, brethren, that you appreciate

those who diligently labor among you, and have charge over you in the Lord and give you instruction, and that you esteem them very highly in love because of their work." In other words, Christians are to esteem, value, and respect those believers who minister to them from church leadership positions. These leaders may or may not be ordained. They may be men or women, old or young, teachers or pastors, unpaid volunteers or salaried workers. It makes no difference. Whoever they are, if they are spiritual leaders, then they deserve the continued respect of those whom they serve. Why should church leaders receive such appreciative treatment? Is it because of their position, academic degrees, standing in the community, age, experience, or wisdom? No. Paul tells us that it's "because of their work." The nature of their responsibilities and the good services they render warrant our deep expressions of respect and appreciation.

2. **Live in peace with one another** (v. 13b). This gift is stated in the form of a command. Notice that peace cannot be maintained unless members of God's forever family *actively seek* peaceful relations between each other. Some of the key things involved in this ongoing process are brought out in these words from Romans: "Be devoted to one another in brotherly love; give preference to one another in honor; not lagging behind in diligence, fervent in spirit, serving the Lord; rejoicing in hope, persevering in tribulation, devoted to prayer, contributing to the needs of the saints, practicing hospitality. . . . Be of the same mind toward one another. . . . If possible, so far as it depends on you, be at peace with all men" (Rom. 12:10-13, 16a, 18). It takes hard and time-consuming work to build bridges of peace. And even though some will adamantly refuse to make peace with us, we must do everything in *our* power to live in peace with as many people as possible.

B. Gifts Urgently Needed (vv. 14-15). The focus in these verses is one of strong exhortation ("we urge you," v. 14a), whereas in the preceding section, the words are couched in terms of a request ("we request of you," v. 12a). Five gifts are presented to us as directives which call for our urgent application.

1. **Admonish the unruly** (v. 14a). Even though it may hurt, there are occasions when Christians should be confronted and corrected with the truth. These times of admonition are needed when a fellow believer is *unruly*—that is, when he or she is undisciplined, disorderly, and irresponsible in

carrying out his or her Christian duty. As members of
Christ's family, we are expected to behave ourselves by
being where we ought to be and doing what we ought to
do. When we become derelict in our Christian responsibilities, God calls on other members of His family to
confront us with this fact and to exhort us to resume
fulfilling our Christian duty.

2. **Encourage the fainthearted** (v. 14a). Those brethren who
   are overly worried, deeply discouraged, or physically
   and/or emotionally debilitated urgently need other
   Christians to lift them up and to encourage them onward.
   This may involve giving them words of comfort, lending
   them a listening ear, or just showing them in some other
   concrete way that someone cares. Whatever the means, the
   hands-on act of encouragement is a wonderful way to
   make a lasting investment in the life of God's people.

3. **Help the weak** (v. 14b). At one time or another and to
   varying degrees, all Christians experience weakness,
   exhaustion, or burnout. When that occurs, they need
   another believer to stand by them as long as it takes to see
   them through. On the other hand, there are some in
   Christ's family who consistently lack the sufficient strength
   to handle life on their own. These weaker brethren require
   the constant, close support of the stronger believers
   (cf. Rom. 15:1). If you are a helper of the weak, keep it up!
   The gift you are giving is sorely needed in the family of God.

4. **Be patient with everyone** (v. 14b). Notice that this gift
   encompasses both Christians and non-Christians; it's a
   family gift that is also to be offered to those who are outside
   God's family. The Greek term for *patience* means "long-
   tempered." It conveys the idea of being tough and durable
   in the face of intense pressure, of manifesting quiet and
   steady strength that can handle disappointment, hardship,
   and pain. Put negatively, God does not want His people to
   operate with short fuses. Anger, irritability, negativity, and
   an unforgiving spirit are not to characterize members of
   God's family. Instead, Christians are called to exercise
   patience with one another and with unbelievers as well.

5. **Refuse to retaliate; do good** (v. 15). This verse states it
   quite clearly: "See that no one repays another with evil for
   evil, but always seek after that which is good for one
   another and for all men." Rather than return caustic
   comments with more caustic comments, frowns with more
   frowns, fists with more fists, and backstabbing with more
   backstabbing, Christians are exhorted by the Lord to

always seek that which is in the best interest of both believers and unbelievers. In other words, we are to return evil with good, ugly remarks with kind words, frowns with smiles, fists with attempts at reconciliation, and back-stabbing with genuine forgiveness. If we would honestly obey this command, historians would be unable to sufficiently record the revival that would sweep Christ's Church and the vast numbers of people who would convert to Christianity.

III. Worthwhile Resources and Reminders for Gift-Giving.

Neither the family of God nor the rest of the world would ever be the same if we who are Christians would just freely and abundantly give these gifts away. But that is not possible unless we possess sufficient resources from which we can draw. God, in His infinite wisdom and from His inexhaustible abundance, has provided us with all the resources that we would ever need. Let's consider three major ones, each of which comes with a reminder that requires our active obedience.

 A. **In God's Word, we have all the truth that we need.** Therefore, we must remember to *read* it.
 B. **In God's Spirit, we have all the power that we need.** Therefore, let's remember to *rely* on Him so that we can effectively obey the Scriptures.
 C. **In God's family, we have all the challenge that we need.** As members of such a diverse family as our Lord's, we have the support and challenge we need to grow in every aspect of the Christian life. Therefore, let's remember to *relate* to God's forever family in a biblical, Spirit-directed way.

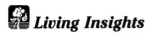 *Living Insights*

Study One

This message gives a list of gift suggestions for the family. But it's broader than "blood relations." It refers to those who are rightly related to Christ—the family of God.

- Paul wrote another letter that mentioned many gifts to give God's family members. It's the letter of Ephesians. Make a copy of the chart below, and turn back to this great letter of encouragement. As you read through its six chapters, jot down qualities mentioned that would affect our relationship with other believers.

Ephesians: More Gifts to Give the Family	
References	Gifts

Living Insights

Study Two

This is a fine list of gifts to give to others, isn't it? Before you attempt to rationalize yourself out of giving these gifts, let's pause to remember the great resources God has provided for us.

- Take this little quiz. Rate yourself in the following three areas by circling the options that best describe your present practice:

1.	How consistent am I in reading God's Word?	Never	Almost Never	Sometimes	Almost Always	Always
2.	How consistent am I in relying on God's Spirit?	Never	Almost Never	Sometimes	Almost Always	Always
3.	How consistent am I in relating to God's family?	Never	Almost Never	Sometimes	Almost Always	Always

- Now, write down two or three changes you can make in your lifestyle to help you further develop these important areas. Be specific and realistic.

61

Germs That Make Us Contagious

1 Thessalonians 5:16-22

The most magnetic people on earth ought to be those of us who are in the
family of God. As Christians, we have reason to be infectiously
enthusiastic—we are at peace with the Lord, have our destiny securely in
place, know the difference between essential priorities and unimportant
involvements, and possess all the power needed to live life to its fullest.
Deep within, there should be such an authentic exuberance that we
couldn't contain it even if we tried. Perhaps a major reason so many of us
lack this winsome zest for life is that we have become far too preoccupied
with the struggles, battles, and demands of life. We need to hear a positive
and uplifting word. We need to know how we can enjoy life rather than
merely endure it. If that speaks to your situation, then perk up your ears!
The seven verses we are about to probe into contain the counsel for which
you have been waiting.

I. For encouragement's sake, some things are . . .

We have a choice to make: We can either spread poison or
encouragement . . . dissension or peace . . . despair or hope. God has
told us what choice He desires us to make through these words of
Paul: "Therefore encourage one another, and build up one another"
(1 Thess. 5:11a). We might reword it this way: "Make edifying others a
regular habit of your life. Be a contagious encourager!" In our last
lesson we explored some gifts we could give to one another that would
spread the germs of encouragement. Two of them were *kindly
requested* (5:12-13). Paul strongly encouraged these Thessalonian
believers to show respect to their spiritual leaders and promote peace
among the brethren. The other gifts were said to be *urgently needed*
(5:14-15). There are occasions when we all need to confront the
undisciplined, put courage into the discouraged, strengthen the weak,
exercise patience with all people, and replace retaliation with acts of
kindness.

II. While other things are . . .

In 1 Thessalonians 5:16-22, Paul continues to reveal the traits that will
make us infectious encouragers. In so doing, he also unearths the keys
for experiencing a life permeated with joy and zest.

A. Continually Appropriate (vv. 16-20). In these verses we
discover three specifics that, when practiced, will cause us to
bear the fruits of a contagiously exuberant life.

1. **Rejoice always** (v. 16). Nothing is more infectious and
obvious than genuine joy. An individual who is truly joyful
cannot help but manifest it. Such people display a
well-developed sense of humor, an optimistic outlook on
life, and a lighthearted spirit. Does joy permeate your life?

Does laughter ring through your home? If not, then perhaps you have allowed circumstances to dictate the way you live. Rise above your situation. Look beyond petty differences and faults. Don't allow your circumstances or the grim responses of others to rob you of a joyful life.

2. **Pray unceasingly** (v. 17). Unceasing prayer will result in a joyful heart. The only way we can have a heart full of joy is to have one free of burdens. And the only way to rid ourselves of burdens is to release them. How can we best do that? Through prayer. How often are we to pray? The text says "without ceasing." The idea here is not nonstop, twenty-four-hour praying but the regular releasing throughout the day of one's load to God. Another way to put it is that we are to pray with the frequency of a hacking cough. When we pray in this way, we will find the discipline to be a source of tremendous therapy and the means to genuine wisdom. Prayer transfers our burdens not only from our shoulders to God's, but it also puts us in contact with God, the supreme Source of all wisdom. No wonder the regular practice of prayer can free us from the anchors of life that drag us down and drain our joy.

3. **Give thanks in everything** (v. 18). Please observe that the text does *not* say *for* everything give thanks. If it did, then God would be making an absurd request, for it would mean that we would have to be thankful for such things as sin and tragic calamities. Instead, we are exhorted to give thanks *in* everything. That is, we should develop and express a grateful spirit as we are molded toward maturity in God's sovereign plan. We may not always understand why certain events occur in our lives. And we may not see, without the aid of hindsight, the good that God is bringing out of our circumstances. But we do have God's infallible assurance that He will cause "all things to work together for good" to those of us who are part of His forever family (Rom. 8:28). That should be enough to prompt us to be grateful in everything.

4. **Do not quench the Spirit** (v. 19). This does *not* mean that a believer can lose the indwelling presence of the Holy Spirit. It *does* mean that a Christian can diminish or even snuff out the ministry that the Holy Spirit has in his or her life. A Christian can hinder the Spirit's work by constantly opposing His prodding, convicting, and persuading work. God's Spirit will not force a believer through the process of becoming holy. Indeed, when He encounters a sinfully stubborn will, He will eventually step away, fold His arms,

and wait for a change of heart. What a barren, lonely feeling to be left alone by God! The nation of Israel experienced this when she continually refused to give up her self-serving lifestyle. The result? God quit treating Israel as if she were a lamb. Instead, He handled her as a stubborn heifer would be handled—He left her alone (Hos. 4:1-3, 11-17). The same can happen to us. But we can prevent this by giving the Holy Spirit full sway in our lives. Among other consequences, we will experience a softened heart toward God, a deeper concern for the lost and hurting, and spiritual power to live a godly lifestyle. These things will definitely help make us contagious!

5. **Do not despise prophetic utterances** (v. 20). Apparently, some of the Thessalonian believers had been downgrading the prophetic revelations that were being presented in their midst. Perhaps this response was a reaction to false prophets who had misinformed the Thessalonians about certain future events (4:13). Whatever the exact reason was for giving this command, the force of it is twofold: (1) don't disparage a true revelation from God, but (2) remain sensitive to God's voice. The same applies to us today. We need to be quick to hear and obey God's written Word. We also need to be sensitive to pick up His counsel to us as given through the timely words of others.

B. Occasionally Uncertain (vv. 21-22). The whole issue of not despising prophetic utterances raises an important question: How can we be certain when it is really the Lord who is speaking to us through extrabiblical sources . . . like fellow Christians, close family, or friends? We can never be as certain about those "prophetic words" as we can about those inerrantly recorded in Scripture. Therefore, with things that are uncertain, we need to "examine everything carefully" (v. 21a)—in short, we must *be discerning.* Just because someone comes to us claiming to have a word from the Lord does not mean we must believe him. God wants us to be spiritually discerning, not gullible. What criteria should we use in our judgments? Paul specifies two things: "hold fast to that which is good" (v. 21b), and "abstain from every form of evil" (v. 22). Anyone who tries to draw us away from the good and lead us toward that which is evil is not acting on the Lord's behalf. Indeed, whatever is genuinely from God will be (1) consistent with His written Word, (2) in line with the lordship of Christ, and (3) in agreement with our spirits. Whatever fails to pass these tests is not from God.

III. Therefore, if you want to be a contagious encourager, then . . .

There are three things you—indeed, all of us—need to do.

A. Remember the goal—to build up others in the Lord.

B. Resist cheap imitations of genuine joy, regular prayer, a grateful spirit, a Spirit-empowered life, and biblical discernment.

C. Release the fear of what others may say or think.

 Living Insights

Study One

This chapter of 1 Thessalonians offers a variety of encouraging gifts. Some of them are kindly requested. Others are urgently needed. And one is occasionally uncertain, while others are continually appropriate. The first on the list of continually appropriate items is to *rejoice always.*

- Let's do a word study on *rejoicing.* Get out your Bible concordance, and make a list of all the references in Scripture to the words *rejoice* and *rejoicing.* (If you want more, go for the words *joy* and *joyful.*) You'll be amazed at how many you will find. Jot down a little summary of the main idea conveyed in each reference.

Rejoice in the Scriptures	
References	Main Ideas

65

Living Insights

The French theologian Pierre Teilhard de Chardin once wrote, "Joy is the surest sign of the presence of God."[1] There's *nothing* more contagious than a happy heart. How's *your* joy? Look over the following phrases and ask yourself how well they describe *you*. Then, ask someone who knows you well to evaluate the same issues in your life. Be prepared . . . you may be taking yourself too seriously!

- I have a well-developed sense of humor.
- I have an optimistic view of today and tomorrow.
- I have a happy, lighthearted spirit that refuses to get its agenda from the morning newspaper.
- I focus on prevention and cures instead of allowing plagues, problems, and diseases to overwhelm me.
- I have cultivated the ability to step back and laugh at myself.

1. As quoted by Bruce Larson in *There's a lot more to health than not being sick* (Waco, Tex.: Word Books, 1981), p. 124.

What a Way to Say Goodbye!

1 Thessalonians 5:23-28

We've been digesting Paul's first letter to the Thessalonians in bite-size chunks. As we have worked through its five chapters, we have come to appreciate Paul's relationship with these early Christians. Repeatedly, we have found this section of Scripture to be right on target with our own needs. Now as we come to the end of the letter, we will discover that even when Paul says goodbye, he provides provocative and relevant truth for us to chew on. So we need to prepare ourselves to confront information that will make us think, turn our attention to the Lord, and show us how we can better live in the family of God.

I. A Brief Review: The Letter as a Whole.

Mothers who have more than one child will often feel something special toward the first one that they don't feel for the others. It's not that mothers love their firstborn more than the ones who followed, but that they develop a unique sense of oneness with the first. The same kind of relationship often occurs in the spiritual realm between a Christian and the first person or group to which he or she sacrificially gives. Apparently, Paul had this special bond of affection with the Thessalonian believers. We have seen this again and again as we have moved our way through 1 Thessalonians. In chapter one Paul gave *thanks* for the Thessalonians (1:2-3). In the second chapter he expressed his *love* for them (2:7-8). A little later he shared his *concern* for their welfare and continued growth in Christ (3:4-5). Finally, out of his love for them flowed *exhortation* (4:1-3, 9-10) and *encouragement* (5:11-14). Obviously, the Thessalonian Christians were very close to Paul's heart.

II. A Profound Farewell: The Writer as a Friend.

When you feel toward someone as Paul did toward the Thessalonians, it can be very difficult to say goodbye. Paul took six verses (5:23-28) to close his letter, and everything that he said manifested his deep affection for these early believers. As we dissect his farewell, remember that God inspired and preserved it for our benefit. So let's contemplate this goodbye with personal application in mind.

A. God, Who Is Faithful (vv. 23-24). The first thing Paul did was to focus the attention of his Thessalonian readers on the living God. And he did it quite emphatically. In the original Greek language, verse 23 begins like this: "Now Himself may the God of peace . . ." By placing the word *Himself* at the front of the sentence, Paul was putting the emphasis on God. He wanted the Thessalonians to know that the Lord—not anyone or anything else—would be the direct source of the good works that he was

67

about to list. Indeed, the God of *peace* would be their provider. In the New Testament, *peace* conveys the idea of harmony, friendliness, and contentment. It's opposed to such things as disorder, conflict, and confusion, and it's void of irritability, anxiety, and impatience. This view of God as the God of peace is certainly foreign to the gods often represented by idols. They are usually depicted with frowns. Their followers are constantly trying to appease their demands and fulfill their insatiable appetites. How unlike the true God—the Lord of peace! His just wrath was fully propitiated (that is, satisfied) by the voluntary sacrifice of His own Son, whose death on the cross provided a sufficient pardon for our sins. In order to gain our freedom from sin, all we must do is accept by faith the full pardon God grants to us through the blood of His Son. There is nothing we have to pay, no work for us to perform, no meetings for us to attend, no church that we must join. Christ has done it all for us. The only thing He cannot do is exercise faith for us. That is up to us—no one else.

A Plea for Peace

If you do not know Jesus Christ as the payment for your sin, as your Rescuer from God's wrath, as your Provider of everlasting peace, then don't put Him off any longer. You will never find a lasting peace with yourself or the Lord unless you put your trust in Christ. Gain the unfathomable peace that God longs to give you. Today—right now—ask the God of peace to flood you with the joy and rest of forgiveness that only faith in Christ can bring.

From God's title, the focus turns to His works. Paul mentions three that he prays for God to accomplish among the Thessalonians.

1. **Complete Sanctification** (v. 23a). The word *sanctify* means "to set apart." In Scripture it has reference to being separated from the roots and fruits of evil. (see 4:3, 5:22).
2. **Complete Preservation** (v. 23b). In case the Thessalonians thought that he was praying for God to sanctify them by removing them from the world, Paul added these words: "May your spirit and soul and body be preserved complete." The Greek word translated *preserved* means "to watch over, to guard, to keep." It often implies assault from

without. And from what or whom would the assault come? There are always three sources: Satan (2:18, 3:5), other people (2:14-16, 4:6), and ourselves (4:3-5, 5:22). The first two come from without and the third one flows from within. The request here is that God would guard the entire being of every Christian *through* every assault of sin, no matter what its source. This presupposes that God intends for Christians to live *in* the world, not *out* of it. The Lord promises to insulate His people through the spiritual battle, not to isolate them from it (John 17:15, 1 Cor. 5:9-11).

   3. **Complete Blamelessness** (v. 23b). Complete sanctification and complete preservation logically lead to complete blamelessness. When the Lord Jesus Christ returns for His own people, they will stand before Him in glory, totally void of fault, condemnation, and guilt. They will be holy through and through . . . entirely free from the penalty, power, and presence of sin. We who are members of God's family have a wonderful future ahead of us. But is it uncertain? Can we blow this happy ending in any way? Not a chance! For "faithful is He who calls [us], and He also will bring it to pass" (v. 24). This does not negate our responsibility to strive toward godliness (cf. 4:1-12, 5:12-22), but it does assure us that God will bring to pass all that He has provided for us in Christ. Indeed, even "if we are faithless, He remains faithful; for He cannot deny Himself" (2 Tim. 2:13).

B. Friends, Who Are Loyal (vv. 25-27). In these verses the spotlight moves away from God and shines on God's people. Paul specifies three traits that are to characterize believers. We could call them qualities of loyal friends. First, loyal friends *pray for each other* (v. 25). They regularly intercede in one another's behalf before the throne of grace. Second, loyal friends are *affectionate toward each other* (v. 26). The exhortation to "greet all the brethren with a holy kiss" is simply a reference to being demonstrative in our love for one another. It was culturally acceptable in Paul's time for a man to greet another man with a kiss on the cheek, or for a woman to do the same with another woman. Today an embrace, a pat on the back, and a handshake would be acceptable alternatives. However, no matter the method of greeting, it is to be an outward expression of our inward affection for other Christians. And it is to be *holy,* without any tinge of immorality. Third, loyal friends *listen to the same body of truth* (v. 27). Paul's letter was written to all the Christians in Thessalonica; therefore, he wanted all of them to hear it. Real friends will keep pointing each other back to the Scriptures. In order to do this, they must hear, seek to understand, and even challenge each other to accurately apply God's Word. After all, there is no finer counsel for a friend to give to or receive from another than that conveyed in the Bible.

C. Grace, Which Is Lasting (v. 28). Paul began his letter with these words of hello: "Grace to you and peace" (1:1). He said goodbye with another reference to grace by stating, "The grace of our Lord Jesus Christ be with you." The root of the Greek term for *grace* refers to things that produce well-being—such as favor, beauty, thankfulness, kindness, and benefit. Grace is always undeserved, immeasurable, unearned, and unrepayable. Theologically, grace is the favor that God has lovingly, lavishly, and endlessly bestowed on people who deserve only condemnation and judgment. This unmerited favor of God has been made possible through Christ, who willingly took our judgment at the cross (Col. 2:13-14). By saying goodbye in this way, Paul was telling his readers to live in the light of God's grace and to enjoy its benefits. What a way to say goodbye!

III. A Final Thought: The Truth as a Guide.

First Thessalonians is not just a love letter that was written by the Apostle Paul to the first-century church at Thessalonica. It is a love letter from the divine Head of the Church to those of us who compose His Church in the twentieth-century. Sure Paul wrote it, but the Spirit of God inspired him to put it on parchment. Thus, every word in the letter is as much from the Lord as it is from Paul. Since that's the case, to disobey or ignore its message is to disobey and ignore the God who speaks through it. On the other hand, submission to its truth is a concrete demonstration of our love for its divine Author (John 14:15, 23-24). Let's not walk away from this love letter without taking the essential steps to appropriate its instruction.

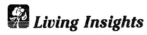 *Living Insights*

Our five-chapter journey has come to an end. It's always enriching to refresh our memories of where we've been in our travels. Let's do a little of that right now.

- Copy this chart onto a page in your notebook. Notice that each of the twelve message titles appears in the left column. Look back over your Bible, notes, and this study guide to determine the most meaningful truth you learned in each lesson. Since we'll talk about applications in study two, concentrate on your *knowledge* in this section. The review should prove to be quite stimulating.

Contagious Christianity	
Message Titles	**Significant Truths**
A Church with the Right Stuff	
A Leadership Style That Works . . . *Guaranteed!*	
The Flip Side of Leadership	
When Your Comfort Zone Gets the Squeeze	
What Does It Mean to "Really Live"?	
Straight Talk about Moral Purity	
Behaving Properly toward Outsiders	
On That Great Gettin'-Up Morning	
". . . Like a Thief in the Night"	
Gifts to Give the Family	
Germs That Make Us Contagious	
What a Way to Say Goodbye!	

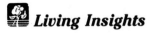 *Living Insights*

Before we say one final goodbye to the letter of 1 Thessalonians, we want to take this opportunity to review where we've been in the preceding messages. Let's see just how contagious our Christianity really is!

- The following chart looks like the one from the first study. But in this chart, we want to emphasize *application.* Follow the same process given in study one, but this time write down the most important practical application you made as a result of each message. What a thrill . . . writing down a series of positive changes in your life!

Contagious Christianity	
Message Titles	**Important Applications**
A Church with the Right Stuff	
A Leadership Style That Works . . . *Guaranteed!*	
The Flip Side of Leadership	
When Your Comfort Zone Gets the Squeeze	
What Does It Mean to "Really Live"?	
Straight Talk about Moral Purity	
Behaving Properly toward Outsiders	
On That Great Gettin'-Up Morning	
". . . Like a Thief in the Night"	
Gifts to Give the Family	
Germs That Make Us Contagious	
What a Way to Say Goodbye!	

72

Books for Probing Further

Contagious Christians may be hard to find, but they are not impossible to develop. First Thessalonians tells us about some first-century believers who were infectious. In so doing, this letter shows us how we can become infectious for Christ as well. Of course, the process is demanding, but its reward is a full and joyful life both now and in the hereafter. What more could we ask for? This series has highlighted several areas that, when developed, will produce contagious Christians. If you would like to probe further into some of these crucial areas of the Christian life, then we would encourage you to consult the sources given below. But please don't substitute a growth in knowledge for maturity in godly living. These materials are provided so that your Christian life might become thoroughly infectious, not simply intellectually stimulating.

I. Toward Contagious Service.

Getz, Gene A. *Serving One Another.* Wheaton: Victor Books, 1984.

Hull, Bill. *Jesus Christ Disciplemaker.* Foreword by Joe Aldrich. Colorado Springs: NavPress, 1984.

Mayhall, Jack. *Discipleship: The Price and the Prize.* Wheaton: Victor Books, 1984.

Swindoll, Charles R. *Improving Your Serve: The Art of Unselfish Living.* Waco: Word Books, 1981.

II. Toward Contagious Relationships.

Crabb, Lawrence J., Jr., and Allender, Dan B. *Encouragement: The Key to Caring.* Grand Rapids: Zondervan Publishing House, 1984.

Hilt, James. *How to Have a Better Relationship with Anybody.* Chicago: Moody Press, 1984.

Inrig, Gary. *Quality Friendship.* Foreword by Erwin W. Lutzer. Chicago: Moody Press, 1981.

MacDonald, Gail and Gordon. *If Those Who Reach Could Touch.* Chicago: Moody Press, 1984.

McMinn, Gordon. *Choosing to Be Close: Fill Your Life With Rewarding Relationships.* With Larry Libby. Portland: Multnomah Press, 1984.

Smith, David W. *The Friendless American Male.* Foreword by Jim Conway. Ventura: Regal Books, 1983.

Swindoll, Charles R. *Dropping Your Guard: The Value of Open Relationships.* Waco: Word Books, 1983.

Swindoll, Charles R. *Encourage Me.* Portland: Multnomah Press, 1982.

Wilson, Earl D. *Loving Enough to Care.* Portland: Multnomah Press, 1984.

III. Toward Contagious Evangelism.

Aldrich, Joseph C. *Life-Style Evangelism: Crossing Traditional Boundaries to Reach the Unbelieving World.* A Critical Concern Book. Portland: Multnomah Press, 1981.

Cocoris, G. Michael. *Evangelism: A Biblical Approach.* Foreword by Haddon Robinson. Chicago: Moody Press, 1984.

DeMoss, Ted, and Tamasy, Robert. *The Gospel and the Briefcase.* Wheaton: Tyndale House Publishers, Inc., 1984.

Eims, LeRoy. *Laboring in the Harvest.* Colorado Springs: NavPress, 1985.

Hendricks, Howard G. *Say It with Love.* Wheaton: Victor Books, 1972.

Lau, Lawson. *The World at Your Doorstep: A Handbook for International Student Ministry.* Downers Grove: InterVarsity Press, 1984.

Posterski, Don. *Why Am I Afraid To Tell You I'm a Christian? Witnessing Jesus' Way.* Downers Grove: InterVarsity Press, 1983.

IV. Toward Contagious Moral Purity.

Bridges, Jerry. *The Pursuit of Holiness.* Colorado Springs: NavPress, 1978.

Glickman, Craig S. *A Song for Lovers.* Foreword by Howard G. Hendricks. Downers Grove: InterVarsity Press, 1976.

Larson, Jim. *Rights, Wrongs, and In-Betweens: Guiding Our Children to Christian Maturity.* Minneapolis: Augsburg Publishing House, 1984.

Lutzer, Erwin W. *Living With Your Passions.* Foreword by Josh McDowell. Wheaton: Victor Books, 1983.

Petersen, J. Allan. *The Myth of the Greener Grass.* Wheaton: Tyndale House Publishers, Inc., 1983.

Rinehart, Stacy and Paula. *Choices: Finding God's Way in Dating, Sex, Singleness, and Marriage.* Colorado Springs: NavPress, 1982.

Swindoll, Charles R. *Sensuality: Resisting the Lure of Lust.* Portland: Multnomah Press, 1981.

Wheat, Ed, M.D. *Love-Life for Every Married Couple.* Grand Rapids: Zondervan Publishing House, 1980.

Wilson, Earl D. *Sexual Sanity: Breaking Free from Uncontrolled Habits.* Downers Grove: InterVarsity Press, 1984.

V. Toward Contagious Leadership and Diligence.

Barber, Cyril J. *Nehemiah and the Dynamics of Effective Leadership.* Neptune: Loizeaux Brothers, 1976.

Barber, Cyril J., and Strauss, Gary H. *Leadership: The Dynamics of Success.* Foreword by Dr. Vernon C. Grounds. Greenwood: The Attic Press, 1982.

Campbell, Donald K. *Nehemiah: Man in Charge.* Wheaton: Victor Books, 1979.

Eims, LeRoy. *Be the Leader You Were Meant to Be.* Foreword by Theodore H. Epp. Wheaton: Victor Books, 1975.

Hocking, David L. *Be a Leader People Follow.* Ventura: Regal Books, 1979.

MacDonald, Gail. *High Call, High Privilege.* Wheaton: Tyndale House Publishers, Inc., 1981.

Sanders, J. Oswald. *Paul the Leader.* Colorado Springs: NavPress, 1984.

Shelly, Judith Allen. *Not Just a Job: Serving Christ in Your Work.* Downers Grove: InterVarsity Press, 1985.

Swindoll, Charles R. *Hand Me Another Brick.* Nashville: Thomas Nelson Publishers, 1978.

Swindoll, Chuck. *Leadership.* Waco: Word Books, 1985.

Swindoll, Charles R. *The Lonely Whine of the Top Dog.* Waco: Word Books, 1984.

Ward, Patricia, and Stout, Martha. *Christian Women at Work.* Grand Rapids: Zondervan Publishing House, 1981.

Insight for Living
Cassette Tapes
Contagious Christianity

Twelve expositional messages drawn directly from the first letter Paul wrote to the Thessalonians. As you can tell from the titles, each study has a remarkable twentieth-century ring to it. Although those Christians lived in another era on another continent, their zeal remains contagious to this day.

	U.S.		
	CCH	CS	**Cassette series – includes album cover** **$34.50**
			Individual cassettes – include messages
			A and B **5.00**

CCH 1-A: *A Church with the Right Stuff*
1 Thessalonians 1:1-10

  B: *A Leadership Style That Works* . . . **Guaranteed!**
1 Thessalonians 2:1-12

CCH 2-A: *The Flip Side of Leadership*
1 Thessalonians 2:13-20

  B: *When Your Comfort Zone Gets the Squeeze*
1 Thessalonians 3:1-8

CCH 3-A: *What Does It Mean to "Really Live"?*
1 Thessalonians 3:9-13

  B: *Straight Talk about Moral Purity*
1 Thessalonians 4:1-8

CCH 4-A: *Behaving Properly toward Outsiders*
1 Thessalonians 4:9-12

  B: *On That Great Gettin'-Up Morning*
1 Thessalonians 4:13-18

CCH 5-A: *". . . Like a Thief in the Night"*
1 Thessalonians 5:1-11

  B: *Gifts to Give the Family*
1 Thessalonians 5:12-15

CCH 6-A: *Germs That Make Us Contagious*
1 Thessalonians 5:16-22

  B: *What a Way to Say Goodbye!*
1 Thessalonians 5:23-28

Overseas Ordering Information

If you do not live in the United States or Canada, please note the following information. This will ensure efficient processing of your request.

Estimated time of delivery: We ask that you allow approximately twelve to sixteen weeks for delivery by surface mail. If you would like your order sent airmail, the length of delivery may be reduced. All orders will be shipped from our office in Fullerton, California.

Payment options: Due to fluctuating currency rates, we can accept only personal checks made payable in U.S. funds, international money orders, Visa, and MasterCard in payment for materials ordered. If the amount of your check or money order is less than the amount of your purchase, your check will be returned so that you may place your order again with the correct amount. All orders must be paid in full before shipment can be made.

Returned checks: There is a $10 charge for any returned check (regardless of the amount of your order) to cover processing and invoicing.

Postage and handling: Please add to the amount of purchase the postage cost for the service you desire. All orders must include postage based on the chart below.

Purchase Amount		Surface Postage	Airmail Postage
From	To	Percentage of Order	Percentage of Order
$ .01	$15.00	40%	75%
15.01	75.00	25%	45%
75.01	or more	15%	40%

Guarantee: Our tapes are guaranteed for ninety days against faulty performance or breakage due to a defect in the tape. For best results, please be sure your tape recorder is in good operating condition and is cleaned regularly.

Mail your order or inquiry to the following address:

Insight for Living
Sales Department
Post Office Box 4444
Fullerton, CA 92634

Quantity discounts and gift certificates are available upon request.

Order Form

Please send me the following cassette tapes:

The current series: ☐ CCH CS Contagious Christianity

Individual cassettes: ☐ CCH 1   ☐ CCH 2   ☐ CCH 3   ☐ CCH 4
                        ☐ CCH 5   ☐ CCH 6   ☐ CCH 7   ☐ CCH 8
                        ☐ CCH 9   ☐ CCH 10 ☐ CCH 11 ☐ CCH 12

I am enclosing:

$_____   To purchase the cassette series for $34.50
              which includes the album cover

$_____   To purchase individual tapes at $5.00 each

$_____   Total of purchases

$_____   **Overseas residents please add appropriate postage**
              (See postage chart under "Overseas Ordering Information.")

$_____   As a gift to the Insight for Living radio ministry

$_____   **Total amount due (Please do not send cash.)**

Form of payment:

☐ Check or money order made payable to Insight for Living
☐ Credit card (Visa or MasterCard only)
If there is a balance: ☐ apply it as a donation   ☐ please refund

---

Credit card purchases:
☐ Visa   ☐ MasterCard number _____
Expiration date _____
Signature _____
We cannot process your credit card purchase without your signature.

Name _____

Address _____

_____

City _____

State/Province _____ Zip/Postal code _____

Country _____

Telephone (_____) _____ Radio station ___ ___ ___ ___

Should questions arise concerning your order, we may need to contact you.